Premarital
Agreements

Also by Joseph P. Zwack

Annulment: Your Chance to Remarry
Within the Catholic Church

Premarital Agreements

When, Why, and How to Write Them

Joseph P. Zwack

PERENNIAL LIBRARY

Harper & Row, Publishers, New York
Cambridge, Philadelphia, San Francisco, Washington
London, Mexico City, São Paulo, Singapore, Sydney

PREMARITAL AGREEMENTS. Copyright © 1987 by Joseph P. Zwack. All rights reserved. Printed in the United States of America. No part of this book may be used or reproduced in any manner whatsoever without written permission except in the case of brief quotations embodied in critical articles and reviews. For information address Harper & Row, Publishers, Inc., 10 East 53rd Street, New York, N.Y. 10022. Published simultaneously in Canada by Fitzhenry & Whiteside Limited, Toronto.

FIRST EDITION

Designer: Erich Hobbing

Copy editor: Rick Hermann

Library of Congress Cataloging-in-Publication Data

Zwack, Joseph P.
 Premarital agreements.

 Includes index.
 1. Antenuptial contracts—United States—Popular works. I. Title.
KF529.Z9Z93   1987   346.7301'6   86-46113
                         347.30616
ISBN 0-06-055072-4   87 88 89 90 91 MPC 10 9 8 7 6 5 4 3 2 1
ISBN 0-06-096181-3 (pbk.) 87 88 89 90 91 MPC 10 9 8 7 6 5 4 3 2 1

To my wife, Paula

Contents

Introduction

We've all heard the horror stories. As the number of divorces and remarriages has increased, there has been a mushrooming of tales about unfair, sometimes bizarre, applications of inheritance laws.

For example:

- A widower remarries. His own children from the first marriage end up with nothing when he dies because his new spouse (and possibly her children) receives everything.
- Man divorces wife, marries his pretty young secretary. New family inherits all.
- Husband dies, leaving wife large insurance proceeds. She remarries. When she dies her new husband (and eventually his children by his first marriage) receives all. Thus, children of the man who died leaving substantial insurance benefits get zero.
- Rich old bachelor with one foot in the grave marries ambitious young housekeeper, nurse, or friend. Bachelor's brothers, sisters, nieces, nephews, and friends who have held his hand and cared for him over the years are forced to take a backseat to the young "interloper" when the old codger soon dies.
- Ugly-duckling daughter has nothing going for her but lots of mommy and daddy's money. Calculating Casanova invests a few years in marriage to the grateful gal and then files for divorce, seeking big property settlement.
- Wealthy older man marries. He writes a will after the mar-

riage, thinking he has provided well for his youthful wife. At his death a few years later, though, the young woman elects to "take against" the provisions of the will. She insists upon a full statutory share for her brief marriage, thus forcing the sale of a long-held family business.

There are dozens of variations on the theme. All are based upon what is thought to be the basic unfairness which results when a newcomer or outright carpetbagger ends up with a sizable amount of money or other assets because of a second marriage or ill-conceived first marriage, often late in life. One of the biggest causes of the problem is that no state in the country allows a married person to dispose of his or her property the way he or she wants (unless it happens to conform to the legislature's plan). Whether the public policy behind the rule is good or not, the fact remains: the minute a marriage takes place, the new spouse becomes entitled under the law to one third, one half, or much more of a deceased spouse's estate in most states.

In other words, the law writes an estate plan for you regardless of what you or your spouse might think is right, and this estate plan can be enforced in spite of the most carefully drawn plans which you or your spouse might agree to after your marriage, regardless of the length of the marriage, regardless of any difference in ages of the couple, regardless of the source of the marital funds, regardless of basic concepts of justice and evenhandedness.

It may be that this state-drawn plan will result in a kind of rough equity in certain cases, but in many, many others it is simply way out of line. Illustrative is a national wire-service newspaper article I happened upon while writing this very page of the book. It originated out of Grand Rapids, Michigan, and was headlined locally as "Her Fortune Is Gone." It described how "an 86-year-old woman, recently divorced from a man not even half her age, is out more than $1 million." The woman's lawyer was quoted as saying, "The money was there before the marriage, and it was well in excess of $1 million. Now it's gone."

An extreme example? Perhaps. But it is also an extremely good example of a case in which a PREMA (premarital agreement) may well have either (1) prevented entirely what appears to have been a sham marriage, or (2) at least given the old lady some protection from this apparent rascal after the marriage.

What we are facing today is a quantum increase in remarriages to an extent never before encountered in the history of our nation. Our legal, economic, and social institutions are just not geared to handle the situation.

In round numbers, we are seeing about a million–plus divorces every year and about two million–plus marriages. Hundreds of thousands of marriages are not first marriages, and therein lies a big reason for this new and unique battery of problems now confronting us.

Combined with this unprecedented volume of remarriages is the existence of wealth undreamed of before. Two-paycheck families, pay equalization for women, pension and profit-sharing plans at work, delayed child-rearing, smaller families, inflation, and other elements of modern economics have allowed some married couples to accumulate in just a few years estates larger than their parents were able to scrimp together in a lifetime of saving.

Whether you are a California couple whose $65,000 home has spiraled up to $350,000 or an Iowa farmer who has seen his 360-acre farm increase from $250 an acre to $2,500 (and now head back down again), the fact remains that America's large middle class now has certain divorce and remarriage fallout problems never envisioned before. Family quarrels and intrigues, will contests, probate claims, and general hard feelings now often appear as standard baggage which follow a second or third trip to the altar.

Many of these trials and tribulations might be easily prevented by use of a rather simple PREMA.

But if this is so, then why don't more people use PREMAs?

In truth, there is really no one promoting them. They have no organized or natural constituency. Our laws regarding division of property between spouses, wills, a spouse's election rights to "take against" a will, dower and curtesy rights, and automatic statutory set-offs to spouses (no matter how brief the marriage) were almost all enacted when divorce and remarriage were relatively rare. Everybody—including lawyers, the court system, the insurance industry, trust departments, the banking industry in general—automatically follows established procedures in the event of a marriage breakup by death or divorce. Practices are institutionalized. Nobody wants to rock the boat, even where gross economic inequities result. This is not because of a deep, dark conspiracy; it is just that no one has systematized, no one has grooved, a plan for meeting this new national predicament.

A PREMA, though, would change the script of most of the horror stories.

Among people who have used PREMAs there has been enthusiastic recommendation. PREMAs work well. They can be used in countless situations. Their variety is endless. They can be amended easily. In proper circumstances the benefits are tremendous and the disadvantages almost nil.

A cynic once defined a second marriage as the triumph of Hope over Experience. Perhaps a PREMA can be described as the triumph of Hope *and* Experience.

Would a PREMA work for you? Read on.

Premarital
Agreements

In preparing your premarital agreement, please do not use the forms in the appendix without first reading the explanatory information contained in the body of the book, including the discussion in Chapter 6 about whether or when it would be appropriate to see a lawyer.

1. Answers to the Most-Often-Asked Questions

"If I knew all the right answers I'd be the smartest student in the whole, wide world," said the boy. "Yes," said the old man, "and if you knew all the right questions you could rule the world."

—J. R. Duge,
Tales of a Ginseng Hunter

A FEW BASICS

Just What Is a Premarital Agreement?

In a premarital agreement the parties define their rights in each other's property, either existing or later acquired, often substantially varying property rights which would otherwise arise as a result of their intended marriage. By definition, of course, a *pre*marital agreement is entered into before the marriage.

Is a Premarital Agreement the Same as an Antenuptial Agreement?

Yes. Also, the phrase "prenuptial agreement" is sometimes used. All fit under the general category of marriage contracts that are signed before the marriage. For ease, we shall usually refer to any such document as a PREMA (premarital agree-

1

ment). A marriage contract signed *after* the marriage ceremony is a postmarital agreement (POSTMA).

What Law Controls a PREMA? State? Federal?

State law. Because we are dealing with fifty-one separate jurisdictions (the District of Columbia is included), I will not of course be able to list the position of each state legislature and high court regarding every issue at the time you read this book. At the end of the book is included a legal bibliography listing every jurisdiction's laws which apply to some of the matters we will be discussing. I have also cited some of the leading cases dealing with PREMAs in each state, and will suggest the proper language to use in the forms in Appendix 1.

The law is constantly evolving. In this book we will talk about the important principles of law as they touch on PREMAs generally, regardless of state. Only in the state of Louisiana, where the laws were founded in large part on the French Napoleonic Code rather than English common law, does one face a system which might truly seem incomprehensible to the lay person.

Are PREMAs Legal in All States?

Although state laws vary widely, all states allow at least some form of PREMA. All states, however, will strike down PREMAs which violate the basic principles of law I will describe in the next chapter. Appendix 2, the State Laws section, attempts to particularize the law in each jurisdiction.

Do PREMAs Have to Be in Writing?

Many, but not all, states have such a requirement. This question should be moot, though, because as we shall discuss in the next chapter, anyone would be foolish to attempt to enter into, and then later try to enforce, an oral PREMA.

PUBLIC POLICY

Do Courts Generally Look Kindly Upon PREMAs or Do They Oppose Them?

Many courts have stated that marriage contracts are favored in the law. This is based upon the fact that the law always encourages settlements or agreements among people. If the court finds, however, that a PREMA in any way promotes a separation or divorce of the parties, then the document is considered to be contrary to public policy and the judge will often declare the document void, either in whole or in part. Also, it can generally be said that the more restrictive are the provisions against, say, the wife obtaining any marital share after the marriage—even if she came into the marriage destitute—the more apt will a court be to void the PREMA for failure to comply with the rules we shall discuss.

Why Do People Usually Enter Into PREMAs?

Most people are attempting to draw up their own financial plan which, for one reason or another, differs from the plan that the state has drawn up for the general populace. Without a PREMA a married person is restricted in the ways his or her property can be disposed of.

Often a person with some wealth is trying to lock in a predetermined division of property to take effect when the marriage ends upon a death or divorce. Later chapters discuss many of the motives for entering into PREMAs.

Give Examples of the Types of People Who Might Want to Use a PREMA.

Typically, a PREMA is entered into (1) when at least one of the parties has been married before and there is a desire to guarantee some protection to children of the first marriage, (2) when there is a significant age disparity between the parties,

3

and/or (3) when there is a sizable disparity in the wealth or indebtedness of the parties.

Is There One Particular Form of PREMA That Is Used?

No, although some states are very specific about the types of things which should or should not be included in a valid PREMA. As we shall see, there is a great variety of forms and options. Even with this variety, though, certain fundamental principles *must* be followed in every state.

Do the Courts Treat All These Different PREMAs Equally?

No. PREMAs that provide for division of property or waiver of rights upon the *death* of a person are more likely to be upheld in their entirety than those that divide property and waive rights upon the *divorce* of the couple. This is one of the areas where following the rules becomes so important.

In Your Last Answer You Mentioned Upholding PREMAs "In Their Entirety." Do You Mean That Courts Can Pick and Choose Which Provisions in a PREMA They Will Enforce and Which They Will Not Enforce?

Yes, in some cases this is true. If a PREMA comes under legal attack, a judge, depending upon the particular facts and law, can either strike down a PREMA entirely, uphold it entirely, or refuse to enforce the objectionable provisions and enforce the rest of them.

Obviously, the forms and suggestions in this book are geared toward obtaining the best possible results.

Do You Think That the Recent Interest in PREMAs Is Just Another Passing Fancy of Our Modernist Society?

Quite the opposite. Marriage contracts of one kind or another trace their origins back thousands of years. Even today premarital bargaining and negotiations are extremely important in many societies, including the most primitive.

In fact, the free and easy attitude of the Western world toward marriages today is thought by some to be a partial reaction against the "arranged" partnerships of the Old World. It was not too long ago that, even in "enlightened" cultures, marriages were in many instances little more than business arrangements worked out between the families of the parties. The plight of Romeo and Juliet was equally the plight of the Williams and Elizabeths, Alexeis and Svetlanas, and Hermans and Gertrudes of the world at the time. Marriages in which the marrying parties have never, or seldom ever, seen each other before the ceremony still take place in some parts of the world.

In rightfully recoiling from the notion of the old marriage contracts, couples began downplaying more and more the financial aspects that used to be the foundations of many arranged marriages. In point of fact, in the last few decades it has become almost a breach of etiquette before marriage to broach the subject of finances. Perhaps some people felt that such matters might interfere with the more important considerations of unfettered love and the right to do one's own thing.

Nowadays, though, there seems to be a willingness to reach a balance in this area, especially in the realm of second marriages. Many people are realizing that facing up squarely to financial questions—before marriage—makes a great deal of sense.

Should a Young Couple Marrying for the First Time Enter Into a PREMA?

Assuming there is nothing extraordinary about their finances, I see no reason for a young couple to execute a

PREMA. PREMAs solve problems that often accompany second marriages, late marriages, December-June marriages, rich-poor marriages, or marriages of convenience. But, as the saying goes, if the faucet ain't broke, don't fix it. I can even imagine some psychic damage resulting from young couples with little or no assets bargaining about completely hypothetical financial problems, division of nonexistent assets, and the like. I may be old-fashioned on this point, but it seems to me there is a danger that a contract providing for disposal of assets in the event of, say, divorce might tend to become a self-fulfilling prophecy for a young couple marrying for the first time. In theory it could work for the couple who think of everything; I just wouldn't want to think about it if I had no reason to.

Are You Saying You Oppose Young Couples Signing the So-called "Intimate Contracts," or the Contracts Which Deal with Nonfinancial Matters?

The type of agreement to which you refer is not included within the documents we shall be discussing. The aims of such nonproperty "contracts" are primarily social in nature. We talk about these to some extent in Chapter 8.

PERPLEXING POINTS

What if My Spouse and I Later Want to Cancel or Amend the PREMA? Are We Locked Into This Agreement for Life?

Many people are under the mistaken impression that once a PREMA is executed, it can never be changed. PREMAs are often changed after a marriage. Great care should be taken in amending a PREMA (and we will talk about how to do it, with a sample form included in Appendix 1), but you should not hesitate entering into a PREMA for fear of being forever locked into it even though both you and your spouse want to change or cancel it.

What if Just One of the Parties, and Not Both of Them, Wishes to Amend the PREMA After the Marriage?

Assuming, of course, that the spouse who wants to do the changing is the one who originally agreed to take less than the normal statutory share, the answer must be that that spouse is out of luck. He or she is bound. In fact, this is one of the main reasons PREMAs are entered into: A properly drafted PREMA will be binding even though a disgruntled spouse later wants out of the agreement.

Chapter 5 is devoted to the many ways of changing the effect of a PREMA after marriage.

Are There Any Problems That Would Prevent a Later Amendment or Cancellation of the PREMA?

Mental incompetency after the marriage would prevent an amendment or cancellation by the incompetent spouse. This problem in itself should not discourage use of a PREMA. After all, if incompetency arises after marriage, many other problems will have to be dealt with also. For example, it also would not be possible for the incompetent spouse to write a will or codicil, or even make a valid gift.

What if My Spouse and I Want to Keep As Our Own Separate Property the Assets We Brought Into the Marriage, but We Want to Share Everything We Build Up After the Marriage? Is It Possible to Draw Up a PREMA Based on Such a Theory?

Yes, and in fact that general formula is being used more and more in place of the more restrictive all-or-nothing language often employed in the past. A PREMA using this concept (called a Prior Property PREMA) is shown beginning on page 91 in the sample forms in Appendix 1. The options available are practically endless.

7

Can the Signer of a PREMA Avoid His Promises Under a PREMA by Giving Away His Property During the Marriage?

First we must ask: To whom is the property being given? If it is going to the other spouse, then quite obviously the favored spouse will not object. But if, for example, the wealthy spouse begins giving away assets to third parties in order to avoid living up to certain required transfers obliged in the PREMA, legal action can be taken, either through injunctive relief or otherwise, to prevent such fraud.

In certain rare cases either children or creditors may also be able to intervene if fraud is taking place and they have relied on a PREMA in good faith.

Will I Have to Get an Attorney Involved in Writing Up My PREMA?

As I mentioned in the Introduction, by the time you have completed reading this book cover to cover, you will probably know more about specialized questions involving PREMAs than most attorneys. Many attorneys have never written a PREMA. That having been said, though, I must still point out that there are some advantages in involving an attorney in the process, especially regarding questions about local property laws and state statutes.

In Chapter 6 I give some detailed suggestions about how attorneys can or must fit into the PREMA equation.

There are also some advantages in involving independent legal counsel for both spouses. More and more courts are inquiring into whether such independent legal counsel existed at the time the document was signed.

What if the Two Parties Sign a PREMA and Then Decide to Call Off the Marriage? Is Either Party Bound at That Point?

Up until the time of the marriage neither party is bound, because the legal consideration of the agreement—the marriage itself—is lacking. But if either side makes any transfers in reliance on the PREMA under such circumstances, then the transfers can be set aside in court (in the unlikely event that the property is not voluntarily returned).

I Have Heard Something About Recording PREMAs at the Courthouse. Is Recording Necessary for Validity?

No, except in exceptional instances, which I will later describe.

As between the two parties to the marriage a PREMA need not be recorded to be effective. An unrecorded PREMA will not stand up, though, against a creditor or purchaser for valuable consideration, especially one without actual knowledge of the PREMA. In other words, even though a PREMA provides, for example, that the homestead will pass to one of the spouses after a marriage, a purchaser of that homestead from the couple (or even a mortgage lender) will not be deprived of the property if money was given for the property without knowledge of the unrecorded PREMA.

In some states an unrecorded PREMA is said to be void as to everyone except the parties themselves and their heirs.

Couldn't I Accomplish the Same Thing with a Last Will and Testament As with a PREMA?

Absolutely not. A will cannot do the job because in every state the law gives a spouse an automatic right to a substantial portion of the deceased partner's estate as soon as the marriage takes place. Whether this share is called a dower right (by the wife) or curtesy right (by the husband) or simply a statutory share (by either), every state imposes it. Community property rights are also involved in some states. Such spousal shares range in size anywhere from about one third of the value of the estate's real estate to 100 percent of the value of real estate and personal property combined, depending on the size of the estate and the particular state involved.

If a will provides for less than this locked-in amount, a surviving spouse need merely elect to "take against" the provisions of the will, thus defeating it. Once a valid PREMA has been signed, however, one spouse cannot later elect to "take against" it.

Both a PREMA and a Will Spell Out How Property Will Be Divided When the Marriage Ends by the Death of a Party. How Does a PREMA Differ from a Will?

There are several basic differences. First, the mechanics: no particular procedure regarding attestation (witnessing) is necessary for most PREMAs. Although I strongly recommend that a PREMA be notarized or perhaps witnessed, neither is a requirement for validity in most states *as between the parties.* A will, however, has very stringent requirements for witnessing by competent individuals attesting to the signing of the will in the presence of each other and in the presence of the testator.*

Next, it should be kept in mind that a PREMA is a *contract* between the two parties signing the document. Wills, though, do not involve an agreement with another party, and wills can be revoked by the testator without requiring the consent of anyone else.†

---

*Some states do allow use (usually limited) of a handwritten "holographic" will.

†Wills *can* be contractual in nature; however, contractual wills are hardly ever entered into nowadays. In fact many states' probate laws specifically state that two wills signed at the same time are presumed not to be contractual between two parties unless there is an affirmative statement that the two joint

Also—and very importantly—since a will is not contractual in nature it does not require consideration, as a PREMA does.

Another major difference between a will and PREMA lies in the fact that a PREMA must be entered into before a marriage; a will may be entered into at any time.

Further, a PREMA can validly reduce a spouse's claim to a marital share in the other's estate in most jurisdictions. But a will cannot effectively reduce a spouse's share below a certain amount (because of the surviving spouse's right to "take against" the terms of the will).

There are also vast differences in the procedures necessary to put the two documents into effect. With a will you must usually open an estate, appoint an executor, publish notice of the appointment of the executor, publish notice to creditors, file an inventory, pay federal or state death taxes or receive clearance from payment of the taxes, pay executors' and attorneys' fees, file income tax returns, file various reports with the county, state, or federal authorities, and perform many, many other steps in order to fully probate the will. A probate estate is, after all, a separate legal animal, a creature of statute. The PREMA, on the other hand, need not go through such gyrations. It is, simply, an agreement between two parties.*

A will is generally controlled by the laws of probate, and a PREMA is generally controlled by the laws of contract.

Do You Mean to Say That the Terms of a PREMA May Be Carried Out Without Having to Go to Court?

Yes. Although the property covered by the PREMA may well be subject to probate proceedings, its manner of distribution will still be controlled by the terms of a valid PREMA and not by the probate laws of descent and distribution.

---

wills are contractual. A contractual will cannot be changed without the consent of the other contracting party.

*In most cases the property that is subject to a PREMA must still pass through probate, but a spouse's rights under a PREMA are usually treated akin to a creditor's claim, and the property can usually be distributed without waiting until the estate is closed.

Well, Doesn't a Court or Lawyer or Some Public Official Have to Get Involved in Order to Implement a PREMA?

No, not necessarily. And that is part of the beauty of a PREMA. It is "self-executing" in the sense that the other party to the document simply does those things, or accepts those transfers, that are provided for in the PREMA. Depending on just what transfers might be involved, you may or may not want to bring in an attorney to help put particular provisions into effect. But, as we discussed a few questions ago, the goals and procedures in probating a will and putting a PREMA into effect are quite different.

Should More Than One Copy of a PREMA Be Signed? And Where Is the PREMA Kept?

I recommend that PREMAs be signed at least in triplicate so that all involved parties can have an original signed copy. Sometimes signed copies or photocopies are kept with attorneys, CPAs, or in safe-deposit boxes. A PREMA is too valuable a document, though, to simply let lie loose around the house.

Placing a third copy with an independent party is a way of protecting yourself against the possibility that someone might ever try to destroy or fraudulently alter a PREMA.

Should Family, Friends, or Others Be Informed About the Existence of a PREMA?

This depends on your particular circumstances. In most cases I feel it is best to tell the children of the parties that a PREMA has been signed, but it is usually not necessary to disclose all the details of the document. The general question to ask yourself is this: Is the information about the PREMA reasonably necessary for the relative or business associate to plan his or her affairs? It may well be. But unless there is such a necessity I question the wisdom of telling everybody exactly what all

12

your plans are. You may, for example, want to amend your PREMA someday but find that all sorts of people are objecting because they feel you're giving away some vested interest they have in your property under the terms of the old PREMA you disclosed to them.

Do You Have to Be Rich to Use a PREMA?

Definitely not. Problems, of course, are always relative, but the problems an average family can avoid with a PREMA are just as important and pressing for the people involved as are the problems of the well-to-do. In fact, from a strictly economic standpoint, the "marginal need" of the money in question is higher to people of lesser means than to the rich.

You Mentioned Before That the Property Rights Spelled Out in a PREMA Are Often Very Different from the Property Rights That Would Otherwise Arise Under the Law. What Are the Advantages to Having a PREMA for the Person of Average Wealth?

There are good practical and psychological reasons for drawing up a PREMA prior to a second or late-in-life marriage. On the economic side the couple may very well have their own ideas—other than the statutory scheme—about how their property should pass. The *only* practical way they can guarantee that their intentions will prevail after the marriage is with a PREMA. There are dozens of reasons why people would want to adopt various forms of PREMAs, and these will be discussed in later chapters; but what it all comes down to is that the only realistic vehicle for achieving their goals is a PREMA. The fact that we are not necessarily talking about huge sums of money is immaterial.

On the psychological side there is something to be said for people laying their financial cards on the table before the marriage. Possible doubts about the other party's real motives in marrying an older or somewhat wealthier person are surely

13

laid to rest with an effective PREMA. The parties can then enter marriage unencumbered with such fears which, in themselves, can sometimes wreck a marriage.

Also, many remarried couples say that one of the biggest difficulties they run into revolves around the children and relatives of the new spouse. On occasion a bitter wedge is driven between the spouses by in-laws who feel that one or the other is being "married for money," even if the amount is not large. To say that relatives should not become so involved is to ignore the unfortunate reality of the situation. Sometimes such relatives have only the best interest of a loved one at heart, and sometimes their perspective on things is best. Sometimes their fears about a marriage are all too well founded. In any event, a PREMA (even if all the details are not divulged) will usually set most of these fears to rest.

Does a PREMA Always Limit the Less Wealthy Person to a *Smaller* Amount Than He or She Would Have Otherwise Received Under the Law?

No, and once again we see one of the great advantages of a PREMA. It can guarantee that the less wealthy individual will receive *more* than the minimum amount provided to a spouse by law.

Here's a worst possible case. A woman gives up her college education, relinquishes a good-paying job with seniority, moves away from her lifelong hometown, gives up present alimony she is receiving, or otherwise makes a big material sacrifice to marry a man who "promises her the moon." The man gives her hell instead—he transfers most of his property away during his lifetime and then leaves her little or nothing under his will. Even if she elects to take against the will, she's probably been had. How could she have protected herself? With a PREMA.

Then again, a PREMA may not necessarily either decrease *or* increase a marital share, but rather simply provide how the share shall or shall not be taken. For example, a spouse may agree to take his or her share in cash, in an annuity, or in certain specified property rather than in the family's corporate business stock or the farm or the family homestead. The possibilities are many.

A PREMA also becomes very handy when one of the spouses-to-be has a large indebtedness, judgment, or liability of some kind hanging over him or her. By signing a PREMA, the parties spell out in no uncertain terms that the property of the other party is completely separate and unattachable for the purpose of satisfying such debt. So in this case it is not so much wealth as indebtedness that motivates the signing of a PREMA.

It Is Almost Always Advantageous for a Husband and Wife to File a Joint Federal Income Tax Return. Does a PREMA Affect the Right to File Joint Tax Returns?

This is an important point. The right to file joint federal income tax returns is totally unaffected by the existence of a PREMA.

I Am Going to Be Remarried. If I Give My Property to My Children or Put It in Joint Tenancy with Them, Would a PREMA Still Be Necessary?

First, making oneself a pauper will create more problems than it will solve. In some cases it is a good idea to make transfers before a remarriage, especially where family businesses are concerned, but don't give away something you will want back someday. If you do make such transfers immediately before a remarriage, you should give adequate disclosure to your spouse-to-be.

Second, regarding the joint tenancy property, I must again caution you to give proper notice to your future spouse. Point out the joint tenancy property in your disclosure statement. If you nonetheless proceed to set up joint tenancies with third parties before your marriage, be prepared for the worst eventualities: the property might be used by your joint tenants, attached by their creditors, claimed by their spouses in divorce proceedings, included in their estates if they die.

Entering into a PREMA is usually a much better way of protecting oneself against the vagaries of the future than the wholesale giving away of assets.

May a PREMA Be Used to Provide for Division of Assets, Waiver of Rights, etc., When a Marriage Ends by *Divorce* Rather Than by Death of a Party?

A tough question on which to end a chapter. Later in the book we will discuss at length the pros and cons of inserting a "divorce contingency" provision in a PREMA, but until we get there I'll simply give the general rule: Any documents that the courts see as promoting divorce or usurping the power of the trial judges to do equity when a marriage breaks up might be held to be contrary to public policy and therefore void. Courts throughout the land have ruled both ways on this precise issue.

The forms in this book are designed to place you in the best position in the courts on this volatile question.

2. The Law: Provisions and Pitfalls

"Little do you know what a gloriously uncertain thing the law is."

—Plautus

We shall be talking about general rules of law and general rules of common sense. Of course the two are not at all the same, yet in most cases and in most places there is at least some relationship between them. What we try to do is this: come up with the best-fitting PREMA plan for you (assuming, of course, you need a PREMA), and then make the document as bullet- and bomb-proof as possible if and when it comes under legal attack within the various jurisdictions.

WRITE IT DOWN

Even though you might stumble on a sympathetic judge who may in some unusual instance uphold an unwritten PREMA upon, say, a sufficient showing of hardship or unfairness, why buy a lawsuit? You should definitely put the agreement in writing, and preferably in at least three signed copies. Since more and more states are enacting laws which *require* that any waiver of marital rights be in written form, you simply cannot rely on oral understandings in this area.

You should also have the PREMA acknowledged before a

notary public. Even though acknowledgment before a notary is not specifically required in most jurisdictions in order to achieve an enforceable PREMA, almost all jurisdictions require the acknowledgment of any document before it can be recorded. As we shall see later, you want to reserve to yourself the option to record the PREMA. Acknowledgment would be even more important if real estate is involved in the PREMA provisions.

Some people hesitate to seek out the services of a notary public because they fear loss of confidentiality. Even if such a fear were well founded, which it is not, you can finesse the problem. You do not have to allow the notary to read through the document. Remember that a notary only acknowledges that you have signed the legal instrument before him as your apparent voluntary act and deed. Just inform the notary what the instrument is, then proceed directly to the last page and sign it before him or her. Of course, if legal counsel are involved, confidentiality is a matter of ethics at all times.

Illustrative of the idiosyncrasies in this field is the law of Massachusetts. Massachusetts is one of the few jurisdictions that talks about the necessity of *recording* a PREMA. In Massachusetts any unrecorded PREMA is void except as between the parties, their heirs, and personal representatives (which is another way of saying, I suppose, that an unrecorded PREMA *is* binding on the parties, their heirs, and personal representatives).

Massachusetts also requires that a "schedule of the property intended to be affected, containing a sufficiently clear description thereof to enable a creditor of the husband or wife to distinguish it from other property" be attached to and recorded with the PREMA itself, all either before the marriage or within ninety days thereafter. The recording shall be in every county or district where the husband resides and where the land (if any is affected) is located. If the husband is a nonresident, the recording shall be in the wife's last county or district of residence.

The only reason I make a point of Massachusetts on this particular topic is to show that states have differing procedural requirements for the execution of PREMAs.* Rather than list each state's points of distinction as the book progresses, I have instead made notes in the listing of state laws in Appendix 2. Only the state of Louisiana has a truly foreign approach to this subject matter, and that is primarily because of its unique (and practically undecipherable, to outsiders) language and law of probate. Even Louisiana, though, allows PREMAs.

WRITE IT DOWN *BEFORE* THE MARRIAGE

Every valid contract requires legal "consideration." "Consideration" is the thing that induces a contract, whether it be an act of forbearance or a promise. The interesting thing about a PREMA is that the marriage itself is the main consideration that binds the contract.

If the document is not signed until after the marriage, the courts will scrutinize it closely to see if there was any other consideration involved. Even if another consideration exists, the courts will take the extra step to examine whether the consideration was sufficient. This is why it is much more difficult to make a postmarital agreement (POSTMA) stand up in court. It is especially difficult if one of the spouses pledges to give up more than he or she would have otherwise been entitled to under the law. Although some state statutes provide for PREMAs and POSTMAs "without consideration," you should be extremely cautious about drawing up a POSTMA that leaves inadequate provision for a spouse.

The fact that you may have talked about signing a PREMA —or maybe even have had the papers drawn up before the marriage—is not sufficient.

It is sometimes possible to correct an error in a PREMA by a postmarriage amendment. Don't count on it, though. Too many things can intervene. Also, a postmarriage amendment

---

*In point of fact Massachusetts is one of the states that has been considering adoption of the Uniform Premarital Agreement Act, which is a model law proposed for adoption throughout the jurisdictions. If the Act is adopted, the old law will probably change.

requires mutual consent. If a problem has developed and you and your spouse no longer see eye-to-eye on some issue, it will then be too late to amend regarding that issue.

There is no legal requirement that any particular written formula or language be used for a PREMA. Even in states that adopt the Uniform Premarital Agreement Act,* the *form* of the document is left up to the parties. I strongly recommend, though, that you at least follow the general guidelines and principles outlined in this book. It makes little sense to go to the bother of writing a PREMA, only to see it blow up at the pop of the first legal firecracker someday in the future.

The PREMA—by definition, if for no other reason—*must* be signed before the marriage.

Although a number of states have laws on the books to the effect that written waivers of marriage rights are allowed under certain circumstances, whether signed "before or after marriage," don't get trapped into waiting until after the marriage to sign the document. It's a dangerous thing to do.

DUTY TO DISCLOSE

Please keep in mind that a PREMA is something special. We're not talking here about selling used cars to perfect strangers. The courts have consistently held that two people entering into a PREMA owe a special duty of disclosure to each other that does not exist in arm's-length business transactions. Caveat emptor does not apply. An obligation exists to inform a prospective spouse of the assets against which he or she may be agreeing to waive any future claim.

The more disclosure there is, the better will be the chance that the PREMA will stand up under future legal fire. It is a big mistake to believe that just getting your future spouse's name on the dotted line means you or your estate will be home free in the event of a later challenge.

Whenever I think about overreaching by people with a spe-

*The Uniform Premarital Agreement Act will be discussed in more detail later, and is set forth in full in Appendix 3.

cial duty of disclosure between them, the classic situation of Judy Holliday in the comedy *Born Yesterday* comes to mind. Poor, beautiful, empty-headed Judy signed everything her gangster boyfriend thrust in front of her, completely oblivious to all the legal implications. Judy, of course, finally wised up.

The main practical problem with a PREMA signed with a *Born Yesterday*-type disclosure is that it just does not have much value. It might be better than nothing, but not much better.

Before the PREMA is signed, each party should have listed his or her assets, along with the approximate values. Such a listing provides actual, detailed notice between the parties, and makes it extremely difficult for someone to plead mistake or ignorance on this point in the future. If for some reason it is not possible to attach a detailed asset list to the PREMA, the next best approach is to list major categories of assets, together with approximate values. Finally, lacking either of the two foregoing statements, there should minimally be an acknowledgment in the PREMA that each party has been informed of the nature and extent of the assets of the other, along with a statement as to approximate total value of each side's assets.

I do not recommend this third approach, though, because of the danger of misrepresentation, whether accidental or intentional. We must "drive defensively" along this roadway to financial and marital security and happiness. In hoping for the best we have to protect against the worst. What, you might ask, is wrong with making a correct statement of *general* total value, with no details? Plenty, possibly.

What is a worst-case scenario in this matter? Let's suppose Bill correctly states in his PREMA that his total asset holdings are $200,000. But also suppose that Bill makes *oral* misrepresentations to Jane that cause her to sign a restrictive PREMA. (For example, Jane agrees to give up her marital share because Bill tells her that his assets are made up mostly of, say, expensive jewelry, antiques, and collections from his deceased wife. Jane feels these things should go to the deceased wife's children and so signs a very restrictive Combination PREMA.)* If Bill's assets actually consist of large amounts of cash, though, he may have pulled something off that will be very difficult to prove in ten or twenty years.

What's the wife to do when she finally realizes what has happened? Start a lawsuit? Maybe. But again, why buy a lawsuit?

An example of one recommended type of disclosure statement is found in Form 4 in Appendix 1 of this book. Of course even better than this, though not necessary, would be a detailed listing of every individual asset of the parties.

A relatively small number of PREMAs have been written to date in comparison with documents such as wills and trusts. Fewer still have been challenged in court. Even with these comparatively few cases, however, it is quite clear that "failure to disclose assets" is the main ground, or one of the main grounds, for attacking PREMAs in court.

States that have legislation on the subject require such things as "fair," "fair and reasonable," and "full" disclosure of each party's assets. The highest courts in each state have required at least as much, even in the absence of a statute on the subject.

At risk of overemphasis, then, I give the following advice to anyone who has visions of obtaining a future spouse's signature on a document that hides a party's assets: Don't do it. PREMAs will work, but not if they are abused. If you are afraid to disclose your assets to your future spouse, or if he or she refuses to waive marital rights to such assets, it's best to face up to the problem right now. Don't compound it with a vulnerable PREMA.

INTENT IS IMPORTANT

Every freshman law student learns the contract-law maxim "Intention is the polestar of construction." The courts will construe contracts, including PREMAs, liberally to achieve what the parties intended. The lesson from this, though, is

*The Combination PREMA will be discussed in Chapter 3.

don't beat around the bush with the PREMA language. We should identify the document exactly for what it is; we should state precisely what we hope to accomplish by it; and we should be as open as we can in describing the property that will be covered by the PREMA. At the same time, we should try to avoid all possible grounds for attacking the agreement. In general, the PREMA should be so clear that there will be little, if anything, to "construe" by the courts.

Anyone writing a PREMA should make every effort to stay away from "parties of the first part," unnecessary "wherefores," and as much legalese and stilted language as possible. In the forms appearing in Appendix 1 of this book, no sentence is included without good reason. A PREMA, after all, is no place to be coy or subtle. Say what you have to say and then move on to the next point.

Undoubtedly you will not be able to adopt the forms in Appendix 1 word-for-word, so here are a few rules about adding your own provisions.

First, be concise and be specific. For example, if you intend to refer to household goods, don't use the broad term "personal property"—which could include *everything* except real estate. On the other hand, "real estate" includes more than just bare land; any residences, commercial buildings, or improvements fit within the real estate category.

If, however, you have to choose between being specific and being concise, be sure to opt for specificity. In fact, this is one reason that legal documents often seem repetitive and cumbersome. It's much better to be safe and grammatically awkward than sorry and scintillatingly agile and brief.

Second, resist the temptation to use wishful-thinking language. Lawyers call this "precatory" language. If you intend to give certain property to your prospective spouse, don't use limiting phrases such as "Knowing that Mary will always treat my brothers fairly, Mary shall receive . . ." Or, "Because I am confident Jane will never remarry, I want her to have . . ." Or, "I have made the foregoing provisions on behalf of Sarah because she is a very thrifty person and I am sure she will be able to live off the interest in these investments." What if

Mary, Jane, or Sarah violates these wishes? Were they wishes or were they *conditions* placed on the transfers? And if they were conditions, are they enforceable?

Make sure your PREMA doesn't raise these questions, mouth-watering as they may be for us lawyers.

BAD FAITH: FRAUD, MISREPRESENTATION, COERCION, UNDUE INFLUENCE

If fraud, misrepresentation, coercion, or undue influence by a party is the moving cause of a contract, the contract can usually be set aside at the request of the injured party. As we know, a PREMA is a contract.

Just what amounts to, say, an invalidating fraud will depend upon the facts in each case. The fraud or misrepresentation must go to an essential element of the agreement. You should ask yourself: Would the PREMA have been signed even without the fraud or misrepresentation? Was such fraud or misrepresentation, in legal parlance, an inducing cause of the PREMA?

Coercion, as we mentioned, is also sometimes used as a ground for attacking a PREMA. Coercion does not necessarily have reference to physical force. If either party were, for example, blackmailed in order to obtain a signature on the PREMA, the ground of coercion would form the basis for challenge. And the types of emotional or psychological pressure that might be applied against an individual are almost limitless.

An interesting question: What if one party, at the last moment before the marriage ceremony, states that he or she will not go through with the marriage unless a PREMA is signed? Is this an invalidating type of coercion? Well, this is exactly what lawsuits are made out of. There have actually been a few on this point. The legal test on this question and others relating to coercion seems to be whether or not the coercion was such that the free will of the pressured party was taken away.

Undue influence is a ground that usually involves the violation of a special relationship. For example, was the PREMA signed because of recommendations from a trusted legal, financial, family, or other adviser? The person doing the influencing, by the way, need not always be the other party to the prospective marriage, but, where the ground applies, it often is. Just the fact of engagement to the other party may well give rise to a question of undue influence, especially if the influenced party relinquished all financial decision-making to the party who gains financially by the PREMA.

If there is any danger that someone could reasonably contend that coercion or undue influence was used to obtain someone's signature on a PREMA, strong consideration should be given to insisting that independent financial or legal advice be sought out before signing. Such independent counseling could well be the deciding factor in upholding a PREMA that might otherwise be subject to attack later on.

On January 1, 1985, a law came into being in California which stated that a surviving spouse need merely prove that he or she was not represented by independent counsel at the time of signing and the PREMA would be unenforceable. Bad faith need not even be an issue. Since that time California, which is very active in this entire field of law, has adopted the substance of the Uniform Premarital Agreement Act. But, in any event, where the question of bad faith might actually be raised—no matter what the state—common sense dictates that a high degree of care be taken in this area.

The fact that a PREMA provides only a small or disproportionate settlement for a spouse does not in itself amount to a showing of bad faith. After all, most PREMAs do, in some way, provide for smaller transfers to a spouse than the statutory scheme would dictate. That's why people usually enter into PREMAs. Obviously, the fact that an individual is receiving an extremely small share of a very wealthy spouse's estate will be duly taken into consideration by any trial judge examining the PREMA, but if the PREMA has been entered into (1) voluntarily and intelligently, (2) after proper disclosure, and (3) in accordance with the guidelines in this book, the PREMA will usually stand up regardless of the size of the marriage settlement.

I have a suggestion, though, which is based not so much on legal niceties as on human nature. The best insurance that a wealthy person can buy usually costs little more than some common *fairness.* If you're a rich man and the woman you are about to marry is poor as a churchmouse, perhaps you can afford to be just a little generous—if not in your original PREMA then maybe by later amendment. After all, the poor girl is going to have to live with you, right? (Hey, only kidding.)

MISTAKE

On rare occasions mistake might serve as grounds for setting aside a PREMA. Mistake as used here refers to *mutual* mistake. (Although one-sided mistake is always possible, if a mistake still exists after alleged full disclosure—without coercion, undue influence, fraud, or misrepresentation—the "mistake" is often the result of one party's intent to deceive, and should more properly fit under the bad-faith discussion.) Mutual mistake implies reasonable good faith by both parties. Both were, in effect, victims of circumstances.

Assume, for example, that at the time James White and Martha Black entered into their PREMA, both thought that James had a net worth of $75,000. Neither realized that James's Uncle George had died and surprised everyone by leaving James a half-million dollars in cold, hard cash. Under these circumstances Martha might well be able to set aside the PREMA based upon mutual mistake at the time of the signing of the document. Of course, one of the advantages of using the forms in Appendix 1 of this book is that specific categories of assets and values are required to be listed. The mutual mistake just mentioned in the case of James and Martha could readily be proven by reference to the disclosure statement by the parties. You can see at once, for example, that Uncle George's assets were never within the contemplation of the couple when the PREMA was signed.

Another case where mutual mistake might give rise to setting aside a PREMA: Assume both the man and woman believe they are in excellent health when the PREMA is signed. The poorer party signs a Complete Mutual Release PREMA.* In point of fact, though, the poor person has a serious and latent disease that surfaces after the marriage. If the wealthy person dies first and leaves a gravely ill surviving spouse, what do you think a court in equity will do to this PREMA? Right. I can hear the judge's words now: "Mutual mistake in the inception of the contract."

Please note that in the situation just discussed, the mistake did not involve the assets of the parties at all. Mistake, then, can involve a variety of matters, but to result in setting the PREMA aside, it must be material. It must go to the essence of the contract.

LAWSUITS TO ENFORCE OR INVALIDATE A PREMA

Having rights under a PREMA is worthless without corresponding remedies to enforce those rights. There are two general ways to enforce the terms of a PREMA: injunction and specific performance.

Injunction

An injunction prohibits, or enjoins, an act, and specific performance, as the name implies, requires that the specific terms of an agreement be carried out. Though one is primarily negative in nature and the other positive, both often seek to achieve the same result: to follow through with the original intent of the parties when the PREMA was signed.†

An injunction might be appropriate where an individual sees that a spouse is about to dispose of certain property which, by the terms of the PREMA, is supposed to pass to him or her. An injunction is to be filed *before* the spouse actually violates the terms of the PREMA.

---

*A very restrictive PREMA which shall be discussed in Chapter 4.

†In some states a "mandatory injunction"—a kind of hybrid action—can be used.

Specific Performance

Contrary to the somewhat negative thrust of the injunction, a suit for specific performance can be brought to affirmatively enforce the provisions of a PREMA. Assume for the moment that the spouse mentioned in the last paragraph had already sold or given away the property before the other was aware of it. Or assume a wealthy spouse adamantly refuses to turn over certain assets as promised under the terms of a Combination PREMA. In either of these two cases a specific-performance suit would be appropriate.

How does the court specifically enforce a PREMA? A judge has the power to effect a transfer of assets by court order alone. Usually, though, the court (assuming a proper case has been made) will order the defendant himself to do those acts which are necessary to carry out the provisions of the PREMA. If the defendant refuses, the court then can find the defendant in contempt and, if necessary, throw him in jail until he lives up to the PREMA. Jail would be an extreme penalty for such a civil matter, but the club is always there if needed.

Both types of suit are brought on the "equity" side of the docket in most jurisdictions throughout the land. Equity courts historically allow much more latitude than "law" courts in receiving evidence and testimony. Equity actions are almost always nonjury matters heard before the judge alone. The judge is both the determiner of the law of the case and the trier of fact. The entire judicial setting is usually less formal and technical than, say, a law action tried before a jury.

ACTIONS TO CHANGE OR CANCEL A PREMA

What if, for one reason or another, an individual who is entitled to legal relief does not want to bring either an injunction action or specific-performance action to put the PREMA into effect? There may be options other than just doing nothing. The main options: (1) rescission, and (2) modification. In lay persons' lingo we're simply talking about (1) canceling the whole PREMA, or (2) changing the PREMA by a formal amendment.

Rescission

Regarding rescission, let's assume the case of a wealthy man who had promised to transfer various assets to his wife according to a Combination PREMA but who refused to follow through with the deal after marriage. Upon the man's death the woman is left with the worst of both worlds. On the one hand her deceased husband did not carry through with the transfers she was supposed to receive, and on the other hand he has pretty much cut her out of her spouse's share of his estate because of the PREMA.

Such a surviving spouse may just decide to make a claim for her *full statutory share* of her deceased husband's estate, and if the executor or anyone else tries to prevent her from receiving it because of the PREMA, she will show that her husband never complied with the PREMA. Thus, she argues, the PREMA should be treated as if it never existed. In other words, she is simply arguing the layman's maxim that turnabout is fair play. Since he didn't live up to his bargain, she now wants to spurn the relatively minor assets she would have received under their PREMA and demands instead her full statutory share! I can hear the man's screams from the grave.

As I have mentioned before, PREMAs work well if they are not abused. But if someone tries to cheat, the result can be devastating, as the above strategy shows. A rescission of the PREMA can represent such an immense and fundamental change in the financial relationship of the parties that even the *threat* of such a lawsuit while the other party is alive will usually achieve amazing results in the reluctant spouse's inclination to do the right thing.

If a wronged party waits until the spouse dies before attempting to rescind a PREMA, the legal proceedings often take place in probate court in a special hearing on the question.* If the rescission action is brought while the other party is still alive, the suit, like suits for injunction or specific performance, will probably be heard in a court of equity.

Modification

Of what use, then, is the modification option mentioned above? Well, perhaps a spouse is perfectly willing to proceed with the PREMA after the marriage but simply *can*not, under the existing language. Let's assume that circumstances have changed and compliance with the original PREMA terms is now impossible or impracticable; or assume that the terms of the PREMA are unclear or have proved unworkable. *If both parties agree,* they can consent in writing to amend, or modify, the original document to take care of the problem. Obviously, in such circumstances of mutual agreement the court does not have to become involved at all—the parties just draw up and sign the amendment. Amendment procedures are discussed later in the book. If you follow the forms in Appendix 1 there should be few, if any, problems of unclarity. Other problems that arise after the signing of the PREMA are, of course, impossible to predict.

The real difficulty, though, is when the other party refuses to go along with the proposed changes. At that point an action for modification might be appropriate. The court (again in equity) will hear the evidence, examine the documents, and do its level best to try to determine what was the original intent

*If you as a reluctant spouse wait too long to seek to enforce your rights, someone could argue that the doctrines of latches or estoppel apply, or that the statute of limitations has run on your claim. In street language, "you've sat on your legal rights." The court might hold that you should have spoken up when you saw what was happening. Since you did not, and since you (possibly) waited until the old guy kicked the bucket and couldn't defend himself against your claims, you lose.

Of course, there are many possible counterarguments to such a position (not the least of which is that the PREMA was not finally, definitely violated until the spouse died without satisfying its terms), but you should at least be aware of the dangers in allowing the PREMA terms to be violated without objection.

of the parties. Then, if need be, the PREMA might be modified in an effort to put that intent into legal effect.

Summarizing, then, the following legal actions accomplish the following goals: *injunction*, prohibition of a threatened transfer or disposition of assets before it occurs; *specific performance*, enforcement of the provisions of the PREMA after the terms of the document have been violated or someone refuses to carry the terms into effect; *rescission*, cancellation or setting aside of the PREMA entirely, thus leaving open the possibility of a spouse claiming the statutory share to which he or she would have been entitled had it not been for the PREMA; *modification*, amendment of the PREMA, either voluntarily or through court action.

HOW DIVORCE AFFECTS A PREMA

A couple has signed a PREMA and are abiding by its terms. The document may or may not provide for transfers of property between the spouses during their marriage, but at least it implies that it will be put into final effect at the *death* of one or both of the parties. But what if the marriage ends in divorce, not death? What happens to the carefully worked-out PREMA? Is it still given effect? Is it totally disregarded by the divorce court?

This is an area of the law in which considerable confusion and diversity exists among the states. Many states have not yet even spoken on this question. Some state courts have ruled that a PREMA providing for division of property in the event of divorce has anticipated and somehow encouraged divorce, and thus is void as against public policy. Such PREMAs are seen as an attempt to restrict the inherent power of the courts to do justice to the divorcing parties, children, creditors, and other involved parties. Other states (especially in the past when there were "fault" divorces) have taken the position that if the wealthy spouse, say, had been guilty of such marital misconduct that the poorer spouse would have grounds for divorce, the poor and "innocent" spouse should then in effect have been able to renounce the PREMA and ask for more property in the divorce action. Other states have taken an opposing view.

Some states allow PREMAs to provide for the contingency of divorce (by what are called, not surprisingly, "divorce contingency" clauses), and others are adamantly opposed to them.

The major difficulty in trying to lay out guidelines and explain the law in this area is that most of the existing case law was handed down when divorces were decided on the "fault" concept. Today, though, no-fault divorce exists throughout the land. Jurisdictions are beginning to arrive at the following position if there is a PREMA with standard provisions and no divorce contingency clause: The PREMA *will be a factor* to be considered by the trial judge in dividing the property of the parties, but the court will nonetheless consider other elements of the marriage before making any property division or alimony judgment.

The court may, for example, take into account such factors as the relative health of the parties, the age of the parties, property brought into the marriage by each, their relative education, their employment, inheritances of either, involvement with any children, the length of the marriage, and fault for the marriage breakup.

Let us consider the case of a PREMA signed between an older man and a young woman. The woman is to receive very little under the terms of the PREMA when the old fellow dies. There is no divorce contingency clause. Several years after the marriage, she runs off with the young milkman (Do they have milkmen anymore?) and sues for divorce. Frankly, I cannot imagine the trial judge giving the woman much, if anything, more than the PREMA would have called for at the death of her husband. After all, it might be argued, why should the woman receive more in these circumstances than she would have under the terms of the PREMA if she had faithfully stayed with her husband until he died of old age at a hundred?

To give her much more would amount to encouraging divorce, which would be against public policy.

Suppose the woman attempted to ignore the PREMA terms in the divorce action. The court, even though stating that it need not be bound by the terms of a PREMA, would very probably still give the mutually agreed-upon PREMA great emphasis in resisting the woman's request for a larger settlement.

A point to be kept in mind regarding PREMAs and fears of a possible future divorce, then, is that it certainly does not hurt, and in most cases it will be very helpful, to go ahead with a PREMA (assuming one is called for anyway). Of course, if you live in a state that allows divorce contingency provisions, you can insert one in the agreement.

If a state opposes divorce contingency provisions, a PREMA will still be given considerable weight if a divorce occurs. Indeed, some state divorce laws now specifically require the court, in arriving at any property or alimony judgment, to take into consideration any premarital agreement entered into between the parties. A few states have such a requirement even though they would strike down as void any divorce contingency provision.

Why all this hedging about a divorce contingency provision? Why, realistically speaking, cannot two competent adults come to a premarital agreement with the understanding that they will be bound by its terms in the event of divorce?

I was afraid I would ask that question.

Arguably, some such provision would be the pinnacle of logic. It states without question the intent of the parties. Almost all contingencies would thus be provided for. Carried to its logical conclusion, the PREMA could make specific provisions which would be effective in the event of death, divorce, incompetency, or unforeseen financial happenings. No. Too easy. As mentioned before, some courts have held that a PREMA that provides for division or waiver of property rights or alimony upon the occurrence of a divorce is *against public policy because it encourages divorce.* Ridiculous? Sure, but

33

most of these cases were decided at a time when it was much more difficult to get a divorce than it is today,* and there was strong public policy against anything that in any way could have made divorce easier.

The fact of the matter today is that it does not make sense in our no-fault states to say that such PREMA language might somehow promote divorce. This legal fiction is steadily losing ground as new cases come before the courts. Yet the old anti-divorce-contingency-provision position is still probably the majority view today.

I must quote from Alexander Lindley, who is generally recognized as the leading legal writer in this field:

> As society has a vital interest in the preservation of marriage, any ante-nuptial bargain that looks toward, provides for, facilitates, or tends to induce a separation or divorce after marriage, is contrary to public policy and void. Thus any provision in an ante-nuptial agreement for alimony or a property settlement in case the marriage breaks up is generally held to be unenforceable.†

The Uniform Premarital Agreement Act is set forth in full in Appendix 3. This Act, which was approved for enactment in all states by the National Conference of Commissioners on Uniform State Laws, is quite progressive in this area. It states that a PREMA may provide, among other things, for "(3) the disposition of property upon separation, marital dissolution, death, or the occurrence or nonoccurrence of any other event; (4) the modification or elimination of spousal support." Because of its newness the Act is virtually unknown among state legislators at the time of this writing. Within the next few years, though, it is likely to be adopted in more and more states.

The Uniform Probate Code also provides for the waiver in writing of marital rights by couples. Superimposed on both of

---

*There are about 1.2 million divorces and about 2.4 million marriages in the United States each year.

†Lindley, *Separation Agreements and Marriage Contracts*, (New York: Matthew Bender, 1984), p. 90–133.

these sets of laws, however, is (and will be) judge-made law which will protect against unconscionable results.

The basic forms in Appendix 1 of this book do *not* contain a "divorce contingency" clause. Such a clause is included as an option, though, and a "severability" clause appears in each form. The severability clause directly provides that if a provision is held to be against public policy, only that offending provision shall be disregarded. The remainder of the PREMA would continue in full force and effect. If you feel strongly that a divorce contingency would be a good thing in your case, I would advise you to first examine Appendix 2 (State Laws) of this book and then have a local attorney check out the most recent court decisions in your state.

In summary on this point, you must be extremely careful in drafting PREMA language that in any way refers to divorce, because of the danger that the courts will think that by providing for the eventuality of divorce, you are violating public policy by promoting it. Even if your PREMA does not contain a divorce contingency clause, the courts will nonetheless consider the document as a factor in dividing up the property. Often the divorce judge will adopt the PREMA almost entirely. But if you want more than that—if you, at somewhat higher risk, want to try to ensure that the PREMA will be *the* deciding factor in any divorce settlement—you should use the divorce contingency clause only along with a severability clause such as is included in the forms in Appendix 1, and only after checking the most recent local case law on the subject.

In spite of Professor Lindley's opinions about the viability of divorce contingency clauses, case law has shown that things today are not quite so bad. Experience has shown that the category of rights being waived has much to do with whether or not the divorce contingency clause will be upheld. By category, chances of validity would be as follows:

(a) Enforcement of a waiver of future child support in event of divorce: extremely small chance of enforcement. Will almost certainly be held to be in violation of public policy.
(b) Enforcement of waiver of alimony: will probably be

stricken down in most states which have not adopted the Uniform Premarital Agreement Act. Even in these states, which allow such a provision, it cannot cause an "unconscionable" result.

(c) Enforcement of property settlement or waiver in event of divorce: has the best chance of enforcement throughout the jurisdictions, even in states without the Uniform Premarital Agreement Act. This is especially true when applicable to premarriage property.

WHICH STATE LAW CONTROLS?

Entire courses are taught at law schools on the subject of conflicts of law. The general rule to be applied to PREMAs is that the law of the state of the residents at the time the PREMA was signed will control regarding questions of construction and enforceability. But if you have parties from different states, a problem can arise at the outset. Also, the parties may move to another state and the new state may declare that its public policy should control on one point or another. And there's a further complication if the parties live in one state but own some or virtually all of their property in another state. All questions to make lawyers rub their hands with glee, right?

You can avoid most such questions. Simply say in the PREMA which state law will control. The forms in this book contain language to this effect. Even this language will not provide ironclad security, but it's far and away the best we can do in an imperfect legal world.

3. Tailoring PREMAs to Your Needs: The "Big 3"

"She knew more than one way to skin a cat."

—Mark Twain,
A Connecticut Yankee in King Arthur's Court

PREMAs all have the same general purpose: to somehow alter the rights of one or both of the parties in regard to the property of the other. For our purposes, PREMAs may be grouped into three main categories, although there are many variations within the categories. These three main groupings are: complete mutual releases, prior-property releases, and combination releases.

Complete Mutual Release. The simplest and most all-encompassing PREMAs involve complete mutual releases between the parties to any and all rights regarding the other's assets. The agreement covers *all* property, whether acquired before or after the marriage. This form of PREMA is severe in its application: you go into the marriage with your own property and you come out with your own property.

It would be somewhat rare for a typical young couple with modest assets and marrying for the first time to enter into any form of PREMA, and rarer still for them to enter into a Complete Mutual Release PREMA. At the other end of the age scale, though, an old couple entering into, say, a marriage of

37

mutual convenience might very well consider a complete mutual release. Because they anticipate a limited number of years together there may be no pressing need or desire to rely on the other for financial support. Whatever assets each person owns are likely to have been built up over the years with the help of another spouse. There are their grown-up families to consider. Think of the reverberations if Mom or Dad suddenly did something that drastically changed the financial scheme of things.

Today, a number of elderly couples are marrying not only for companionship but also for mutual cost-sharing in living arrangements. A few people admit to marrying for tax purposes only. There are deathbed marriages and marriages for the sole purpose of "giving a child a name." There are some marriages for immigration-law purposes, marriages to avoid having to testify against a spouse, and marriages for various other reasons not having a thing to do with mutual love and a desire to assume the responsibilities of marriage. Whatever the motivation, if the marriage is primarily one of convenience, it might well be a good candidate for a Complete Mutual Release PREMA.

Use of the phrase "marriage of convenience" does not imply, by the way, that such marriage does not involve love between the parties; it is just that the parties in such unions are often concerned with matters which do not involve romance or starting a new family.

There is no hard-and-fast reason why a PREMA must involve a "mutual" release; it could be a unilateral, or one-sided, release. However, it makes little sense to try to put into effect a one-sided release that allows the wealthy party to give up nothing. We *know* that in a Complete Mutual Release PREMA the less wealthy party is going to be asked to give up all claim to the property of the wealthy party, so what can be gained by the wealthy party not giving up all rights to the (nonexistent or minimal) assets of the poorer partner? A one-sided PREMA that gives the rich person even more is just not logical. It gratuitously brings into question, in fact, whether there might have been some type of fraud, duress, or mistake involved with the PREMA.

On the question of the mutuality of the PREMA release, then, the lesson is this: if the poorer party is giving up all claims to the other's property, make sure the document has reciprocal, or mutual, provisions releasing claims by the wealthier spouse.

A sample form of a Complete Mutual Release PREMA is found in Appendix 1 of the book at page 88.

Prior-Property Release.   More common today than the Complete Mutual Release PREMA is an agreement that allows each party to keep his or her own assets accumulated *prior* to the contemplated new marriage, but permits the parties to share in the accumulations that they jointly build up after the marriage.

There are good reasons for having such a PREMA. First, if either party comes into the second marriage with assets that everyone recognizes should rightfully pass to the children by a prior marriage, this form of PREMA allows such intent to be put into effect. Second, there is a strong psychological basis for this concept in a second marriage. A Prior Property PREMA allows the parties to say, in effect, "We weren't partners before, but we're full partners in everything now." With this type of PREMA there need be no financial holding back in anything done after the marriage. Such a PREMA promotes a bonding of the parties in a second marriage by the commingling of jointly created new assets. Certain other PREMAs, which usually require separation of financial lives, sometimes also unfortunately result in a separation or distancing in the personal lives of the couple.

A good economic rationale has also been offered for this form of PREMA. Such a PREMA is particularly helpful when both parties will be working together in some commercial venture or farming operation, or where both parties earn incomes but do not want to have the bother of keeping track of whose income is whose as the marriage goes on.

What type of people would use a Prior Property PREMA? Often they are individuals approaching middle age and, unlike the profile of the complete mutual release users, they are not marrying primarily for convenience. They are of an age so as to anticipate a relatively long marriage and in many cases may even be considering having children of their own. The fact that a child or children may become a part of the family picture only adds strength to their general belief that Day One of the marriage is also the first day of the rest of their economic lives together as a full partnership.

Because people who sign Prior Property PREMAs will not be making claim to the assets owned by the other party prior to the marriage, extra care must be taken to list exactly the assets that each side brings into the marriage. This does not mean that even the smallest items with no value must be specified,* but the list should nevertheless be complete.

It should also be made clear in the PREMA whether substitutions of prior assets are to be included or not. Oftentimes they are, so that their equivalent value can be set aside when the time comes. For example, Mary brings an automobile worth $10,000 into the marriage. Obviously, she will not put the car in storage during the marriage. She will use it, and if at the time of husband Fred's death the replacement vehicle is worth $15,000, then so be it; she will be able to claim $15,000's worth of car. She came into the marriage with a certain make of car in good condition and, under the prior-property theory, is entitled to retain an asset or its equivalent as a part of the property she had acquired before the marriage. (Actually, since cars are separately titled, they often do not prove to be a problem because they are likely to continue to be registered in separate names during the marriage. The "substitution" question applies, though, to all assets.)

What about the *income* from prior-held property after a marriage? Is it received separately or is it thrown into the

---

*Rather than list every individual item with a value less than, say, fifty or a hundred dollars, such items are often lumped into a miscellaneous category and given a value. If the couple wants to list even the little items, the "miscellaneous" category can contain a separate attached list.

family pot of after-marriage property? It all depends on what the couple wants to do. The point is, you should take the question out of the matter and simply state in the Prior Property PREMA what your choice is. I can think of strong considerations on both sides of this particular question. The simplest solution, of course, would be to throw the interest, dividends, and other property-generated income into the family pot as the marriage progresses, and only consider the stocks, bonds, certificates, and the like as prior property. Then what about stock splits? Should they be considered prior property or income? Again, spell it out.

If the parties maintain separate accounts on all assets, and their dividends, interest, stock splits, trades, and the like are reinvested and never commingled, the problem is somewhat more easily dealt with. But complete separation of later-acquired income is often difficult when both premarital separate assets and postmarital joint assets are involved. Remember that you will probably be filing joint federal income tax returns after your marriage. Your spouse is, either directly or indirectly, paying income tax on your income even if you receive it as separate property after the marriage.

It may well be, of course, that the parties own very little personal property but instead have, say, real estate holdings. How are improvements to the real estate after the marriage to be treated? The Prior Property PREMA assumes that any improvements in real estate will be made with prior-property funds of the owner of the real estate, and therefore the improvements will remain a part of the real estate retained by the owner. But if the funds for improvements after the marriage come from joint income of the couple, an amendment of the PREMA might be in order so as to give the contributing spouse some interest in the improved property.

By the same token, if an individual's wealth consists almost entirely of one large block of stock of a certain company and the company merges and trades or splits shares, this entire question about defining after-acquired income merits more than casual treatment.

The above are a few examples where the tailoring of

PREMAs becomes important. Don't be afraid to add a sentence here and there to the Appendix 1 forms. Make the PREMA conform to your situation. It is surprising how many potential pitfalls can be avoided by this tailoring process. Then, after the marriage, when the parties discover that some of the anticipated difficulties did not surface at all—but other, unforeseen, difficulties might have arisen—amendments can possibly be used. But, as I have suggested earlier in the book, if there is no basic PREMA structure at all on which to perform such minor operations, then there is the danger that some rather innocuous-appearing little financial mite will someday develop the horns, claws, and teeth of a monster.

I have encouraged the use of a Prior Property PREMA on many occasions. It is especially helpful when, for example, a young or middle-aged widow enters a second marriage owning substantial assets which have arisen only because of life insurance benefits, wrongful-death benefits, inheritance, or some other such source from the deceased spouse alone. Obviously, the inducement for using such a PREMA would be even stronger if the deceased spouse has surviving children who should be protected financially.

It has been my experience that once the matter is brought up for discussion, most spouses-to-be have no objection to signing a Prior Property PREMA when there are such top-heavy financial considerations on the other side. In fact, they often seem quite eager to prove that they want to protect their new spouse and the children of the former marriage with such an agreement.

As always, some fairness on both sides will go a long way toward heading off possible conflicts.

One area that causes concern among the best-intentioned people is the marital home. After the marriage the new family often chooses to occupy the existing home of one of the parties. Let's say everyone agrees that the home should be considered as "prior property" to be retained by the owner. But there is something foreign about cleaning, painting, wallpapering, repairing, and spending every day of one's life in a house owned by the other party alone. The non-owner spouse often wants to feel like more than a mere tenant in the house. One solution involves deeding over a half interest in the home to the non-owner spouse in return for a lien or a note and mortgage equal to the value of the half interest in the property. The no-interest note is not payable until the death of the prior-owner spouse, or sale of the home.*

As the years go by—and especially if the couple is young enough to have their own children—the evolving relationship of the parties can be taken into consideration by PREMA amendment or even termination.

An example of the Prior Property PREMA is found beginning on page 91 of Appendix 1. Be sure to note the various options available with this kind of PREMA, and don't hesitate to further tailor the document to your needs.

Combination Release. The Combination PREMA gives the greatest possibilities for variety. The options are almost endless. It has elements of both of the PREMAs already discussed. Both of the other PREMAs mentioned previously involve all-or-nothing principles. As we saw, the complete mutual release requires each party to give up *all* rights to his or her spouse's property, while the prior-property release involves giving up *all* claims to the other's premarriage property but allows a sharing in *all* property acquired after the marriage. So, even though the Prior Property PREMA allows much, much more flexibility than the complete mutual release, the Combination PREMA is more flexible still.

In a Combination PREMA the less wealthy spouse-to-be usu-

---

*It is doubtful that a presently taxable event for the "seller" occurs in such a transaction because (1) the note is not payable at any ascertainable time, (2) there would be no gift tax payable because of the unlimited marital deduction available to the spouses, and (3) there may never be *any* tax upon sale of the house because of the after-age-fifty-five exclusion. A tax adviser should be consulted on this point if this procedure is used.

Of course, instead of signing a note, the non-owner spouse could make a transfer into joint assets of property with similar value, thus achieving a trade. This would probably not qualify as a "like-kind" transfer under Internal Revenue Code provisions unless the trade involved an interest in another house.

ally gives up all statutory and dower rights to the other's property in return for some type of payment, which is usually less than the law would otherwise have required. The payment is usually either a lump sum, a monthly payment for life or a fixed number of years, insurance policy proceeds, or a combination of money and property. A Combination PREMA is the most complicated of the Big 3 and is more apt to be used by wealthier individuals and those faced with the most sophisticated financial holdings.

For the right person, the advantages of a Combination PREMA are several. Its main appeal is that it allows a person of wealth to retain control of most of his assets but at the same time assures that the spouse will be provided for adequately. The following are factors which would tend to encourage the signing of a Combination PREMA, any one (or more) of which might in itself be enough to tip the scales:

1. The two parties agree that the less wealthy spouse has no requirement for great sums of money after the death of the wealthy spouse;
2. The poorer spouse has little or no experience handling large sums of money;
3. The poorer spouse is well satisfied receiving, say, an annuity or other payments sufficient for personal needs during the rest of his or her life;
4. The main source of wealth of the rich spouse is a family business, estate, farm, or other income-producing property, which should, in fairness, be passed on down to children or those who have been active in working with the business or asset over the years;
5. The parties agree that whereas a complete mutual release would not leave the poorer surviving spouse with enough assets (possibly none) to live on, the prior-property agreement would actually provide for the transfer of too many assets to the poorer spouse.

In some cases a Combination PREMA may result in the poorer spouse receiving *more* than he or she would otherwise have received under the law, but the PREMA accomplishes some other purpose, such as preventing the breakup of a business or particular investment holding. So remember that the Combination PREMA allows people, if they wish, to provide for all sorts of nonmonetary objects in addition to the monetary objects of the agreement. Although the final result may or may not exceed what the poorer spouse would have received by taking his or her statutory or dower share, in the large majority of cases the ultimate share will be less.

Just a few examples of the things that a Combination PREMA may provide for: On the death of husband Tom, wife Sally shall (a) sell the long-held family residence to her stepson William for its appraised market value; (b) transfer shares of stock in the family business to her step-daughter Ellen for its book value; (c) transfer the lake cottage to brother-in-law George, while retaining a life tenancy in the property; (d) receive a life tenancy in the family's condominium; (e) receive monthly income from Tom's testamentary trust in the amount of x dollars, with annual cost-of-living increases; and/or (f) receive the proceeds of a life insurance policy in which Sally is named as beneficiary.

In consideration of such provisions Sally releases all other rights and claims to husband-to-be Tom's estate.

Often, Combination PREMAs are as simple as this: in consideration of the mutual releases of the spouses to any claim against the estate and assets of the other, the wealthier spouse agrees to take out and maintain a new term-life-insurance policy on his life payable to the poorer spouse in an amount of, say, $250,000. Or an existing policy could be transferred over. Or an item of real or personal property could be transferred over. Of course, the possibilities go on and on.

An example of Combination PREMA provisions is found beginning on page 94 of Appendix 1.

The Big 3 give you almost every possible chance to cover your individual circumstances. If you follow the guidelines in Appendix 1 and keep in mind the general rules mentioned in the last chapter regarding insertion of your own provisions when called for, you will have the basic framework for practically any PREMA.

4. Think Before You Sign

"Make haste slowly."

—Augustus Caesar

Since the person being requested to enter into a PREMA is most often the younger of the two, he or she is also probably the less experienced in business matters. Therefore, maximum caution should be the order of the day before signing any papers.

As we have already seen, there may be many reasons to sign a PREMA; but let's look at the "other side" of some typical situations.

First of all, suppose that you as a young person are asked to sign a PREMA by a spouse-to-be who is substantially older or in poor health. The rationale advanced for the document is that it would be grossly unfair, for goodness sake, for you to drop in during the last few years of the spouse's life and reap the financial benefits that took a lifetime to build.

It is true that the marriage may not last long because of the health or age factor. It is also true, though, that a very large portion of your married time could be used nursing the other party during the most unhealthful years of his or her life. You may gladly do this because of your love for the older person, but keep in mind that you may never have any counterbalancing years of good times which same-age couples often enjoy.

It may be easy indeed for your pros ective in-laws to think of you as a Johnny- or Janie-come-lately, but then who will be caring for your spouse on an everyday basis? Who indeed. Of course it will be you, during all of which time the in-laws just *might* visit your spouse a couple of times a year. Their lives will be sailing along smoothly while you, "come-lately" type that you are, put your time in in the trenches. Although no one wants to be accused of marrying someone simply for money, it makes little sense to go to the opposite extreme and place yourself in a position of low-paid nursemaid merely to prove your honorable intentions to the world.

So if you are a young person, you should be extremely careful about being shamed into signing a total giveaway of your marital rights. A Complete Mutual Release PREMA should usually be avoided. All things considered, a Combination PREMA should be able to take care of the situation nicely.

Next assume the case of the young woman who is to be married to the businessman who has "been stung once and doesn't want to get stung again." In the young woman's eagerness to show her good faith she pledges that her only interest is the love and affection of her husband-to-be. Love will conquer all. Material things mean nothing to her, so she signs an extremely restrictive PREMA. Sounds all well and good. But if the two of them are of about the same age and may well live the next twenty-five years or so together, why, one might ask, should the woman not share in the wealth she helps her husband accumulate over the next decades? This situation might be a good one for using the future financial partnership concept inherent in a Prior Property PREMA.

What about a case in which the parties have lived together for some time before the marriage, or where one party has performed valuable services for the other (no, not just *that*) over the years? Perhaps the spouse-to-be has already helped accumulate assets or relieved the other of financially burdensome wages which would otherwise need to have been paid to strangers. The question thus becomes: Should the valuable services before the marriage be completely disregarded by the wealthy spouse now requesting a PREMA? Obviously the answer is no. This does not mean that *no* PREMA should be signed, but the kind of document to be used must, to be fair, take such things into consideration.

Even the list of assets owned by the parties at the time of signing of the PREMA would be affected by such prior living or working arrangement. Let's say that the woman has worked full-time or part-time in her fiancé's business for a period of years without pay. If assets are listed based solely on title to the property, the man will be shown owning a 100 percent interest in the business even though the woman's contribution may have made the difference between success or failure of the business during the past years. In such a case a value should be written in the woman's list showing her contribution to the man's assets, with an appropriate notation on the man's listing of assets regarding such contribution.

Let us assume a scenario in which a young woman entering her career after college is asked to sign a restrictive PREMA before marrying a man fifteen or twenty years her senior. He is very well-to-do and has been married before. She has just reached the juncture in her life where she will for the first time be earning real money. She is madly in love, yet the question remains: Should she give up substantially all claim to the man's present and future assets and at the same time cut off her own chances to accumulate wealth while she keeps the home fires burning for her husband-to-be? Many things have to be weighed in such a decision. Will she or won't she be able to work and better herself in her chosen career? Has it always been her plan to marry, settle down, and take over the all-important job of raising children and managing the household? Is her husband-to-be being reasonable in his requests?

The financial point to keep in mind when looking at the situation above is that there should be some recognition of the individual monetary sacrifice being made by the woman. Even though the man has all the assets, some consideration should be given to the fact that the young woman will be stunting her earning opportunity to have reached the same asset level as the man in fifteen or twenty years. A highly restrictive Complete Mutual Release PREMA may not be the

PREMA of choice for the woman in such a case. She should probably opt for a liberal Combination or even a Prior Property PREMA.*

The basic approach in all of the foregoing examples has to be one of fairness and a balancing of interests. If you are asked to sign a PREMA, one of the questions to be posed is, who is the spouse trying to protect? Himself? Children by a former marriage? Aged parents in a nursing home? A second cousin he never sees?

Is he really afraid of a divorce and actually trying to protect himself to some degree from a big property-settlement demand you might make later on? What is *your* track record for marriage stability? Did you have a prior marriage or marriages that ended in divorce? All these are valid questions. If there has been a prior marriage for either of you (whether it has ended in divorce or death of a spouse), a PREMA may in fact be exactly what is called for. But here's the stickler: Is the PREMA *reasonable* under all the circumstances? You now know that there are premarital agreements and there are premarital agreements. Since they are as different as night and day, work toward a fair document. If you can't arrive at a fair document, then don't sign it—and that's all there is to it.

It may very well be that you should—horror of horrors— seek the advice of a lawyer when your future spouse presents a PREMA to you. This would be especially true in the unlikely event the other party advises against seeing a lawyer. Also, if you do not understand the document or if it contains large amounts of legal verbiage or strange-sounding phrases, legal advice would be called for. The place for lawyers in this whole scheme of things will be discussed in Chapter 6.

---

*A Prior Property PREMA may not be too bad a financial deal for the woman. If she shares in all future income and asset accumulations of her spouse, she will be starting with a much higher base for increasing wealth than if she and an impecunious young man had started out together and shared their income and assets as time went on. Statistically, she will outlive a man who is fifteen or twenty years older than she is by about twenty to thirty years.

Are you on good terms with your future in-laws? If not, be doubly cautious, because they are the ones you will be dealing with if something happens to your spouse. It's bad enough when children of a former marriage make a parent's second marriage miserable; it's even worse when those same children carry the battle past the marriage, past the gravesite, and into a war of attrition with the surviving spouse under the terms of an unworkable PREMA.

If in this entire discussion I fail to mention the importance of trust, love, and loyalty, it is of course not because they are unimportant. But there are hundreds of books that counsel about such things in marriage. I am sure you would not be reading this book if you seek advice primarily in such areas. You are reading this because you want to know the pros and cons of a specialized area of contract law that could directly affect your financial security for the rest of your life. So if my advice seems a bit calculative and unromantic, I will accept such criticism if I can at the same time manage, within the limitations of this rather brief written volume, to give you some effective legal guidelines for PREMAs.

Sometimes questions about entering into a PREMA arise naturally in a couple's premarriage plans. Other times, though, the entire subject is never broached, even though one of the parties wants very much to discuss it. Should that person simply hide his feelings, hoping for the best? Of course the question almost answers itself, and the answer is an emphatic no. Your PREMA discussion is a bit like the required birds-and-bees talk that parents have to face up to. It's best to get it over with and go on to other things. Everyone will feel better once the topic is brought up and decisions are made.

In approaching such a discussion there are, as in all things, right ways and wrong ways to tackle the job. Anyone who goes at it in an arrogant or condescending or accusatory manner is off on the wrong foot. (In fact, a mean-spirited person may be so greedy that he ends up insisting upon a document that is, for one or another of the reasons mentioned in Chapter 2, unenforceable in any event.)

Men shouldn't worry about "bothering the little lady's pretty head with talk about money matters." Today, practically all women have worked outside the home; have maintained a checkbook; have purchased items; have paid rent or house payments, utilities, and car installments; have withstood sales presentations of all kinds; and in general have had much the same financial experience as men. None should be too sensitive or protected to talk about money matters. And women should not fear that their man's ego is too delicate a thing to stand the shock of a money talk.

In any discussion about PREMAs please bear in mind that not all questions you will be faced with are black or white. You do not necessarily have to decide whether you will enter into one particular kind of PREMA or none at all. For the second-marriage couple there is often general agreement that *some* kind of PREMA should be signed; it's simply a question of what the document should be. That having been said, though, I must repeat: Don't be rushed into anything. There are many, many choices open to you. Think before you sign.

5. Can You Defeat, Avoid, or Change the Terms of a Valid PREMA?

"Only the very wisest and the very stupidest never change."

—Confucius

For the sake of this discussion we are going to assume that all the proper procedures have been followed between two competent parties and that we have a valid existing PREMA. Are we stuck with the document, as is, for life?

I hate to answer such a straightforward question in such a wishy-washy way, but I'm afraid I must: Yes and no, depending on a variety of elements that we shall discuss.

Amendment or Termination Agreement. Let us examine the easiest case first: A man and woman have entered into a PREMA, married, and as time has passed *both agree* that the document should be either changed or canceled completely.

Here the couple need merely enter into an Amendment or a Termination Agreement. A suggested Amendment is found at page 103 and a Termination Agreement is set forth beginning on page 106 of Appendix 1. What makes this case so easy is that we are talking about mutual consent, full agreement, no adversarial problems.

Even so, a few words of caution.

You must be extremely careful about the way you make the changes in a PREMA. Even the order in which changes are made is important. For example, suppose a man and woman enter into a Prior Property PREMA and then after a few years of the marriage the man decides he would like to increase the amount of property he leaves to his wife. He definitely should *not* terminate the PREMA with the thought that he will later enter into a new agreement with the more liberal provisions in it. Once the PREMA is terminated, it's terminated! There is nothing left to amend. Any new marriage agreement at that point may require sufficient legal consideration, just like the more-difficult-to-uphold POSTMA.

Remember, then: amend first, terminate last. Never the other way around.

So *when both parties agree,* they can effect a change in their PREMA by signing a new document called an Amendment (for a modification), or by signing a Termination Agreement (for a cancellation of the PREMA). The same signing formalities should be followed for these documents as for the PREMA itself, and if the PREMA had been recorded, so also should be these documents.

Outright Gift. Another way to effectively defeat the original terms of a PREMA is by making outright transfers before the PREMA becomes fully operative. In other words, before death, incompetency, or divorce occurs a gift is made.

The most common types of property and the means of transfer are:

1. Real estate: By deed;
2. Bank accounts and certificates of deposit: By the adding of names to the appropriate account or certificate at the bank, savings and loan association, credit union, etc.;
3. Shares of stock or bonds: Usually, by surrender and reissuance. Sometimes they may be assigned or endorsed over on the back of the security itself, but then it is usually best to follow on through by surrender and reissuance;
4. Insurance policies: By assigning or amending. Of course, a beneficiary can be changed by executing a change of beneficiary designation;

5. Motor vehicles: By signing over the certificate of title;
6. Untitled tangible personal property (such as household goods, tools, appliances, art work, collections, jewelry, miscellaneous): By bill of sale. Although most personal property is transferred by simple delivery of possession, questions may well remain about just who did have possession of certain items when two people have been living together. A bill of sale is not *required* to effect a gift of such untitled personal property, but it is an excellent way to prove that the gift was made. Be sure to make physical delivery of the bill of sale at the time of the gift.

Joint Tenancy.   Creating a joint tenancy actually amounts to making a gift to the new joint tenant.

If a well-to-do spouse wishes to modify an existing PREMA without (for one reason or another) drawing up and signing a formal document, he may simply create one or more joint tenancies between himself and his spouse. If the account is institutional, he need only go to the institution and add his spouse's name to it, making certain that survivorship provisions exist. Most joint accounts have the survivorship element in them, but you should make special inquiry just to be sure. Such accounts that say "and" or "and/or" almost always include the right of survivorship. Accounts that connect two names with "or" usually create a tenancy in common (which we will discuss in the paragraph after next). If the property to be transferred is real estate, the giver should execute a deed to himself and spouse in joint tenancy with full rights of survivorship.

In some states a *tenancy by the entirety* is possible. A tenancy by the entirety is (1) a joint tenancy (2) between spouses (3) with right of survivorship (4) without the right of one party alone to sever. Our discussion of joint tenancies includes tenancies by the entirety.

Joint tenancy, which in many instances involves the right of survivorship, should not be confused with *tenancy in common.* In a tenancy in common each tenant owns an undivided interest in the property; there is no right of survivorship; and, upon death, the deceased tenant's interest passes to that tenant's heirs or beneficiaries. To guarantee that the survivorship aspect is included in a real estate transfer, it is required in some states—and is just good practice in others—to use a phrase that specifically excludes the possibility of a tenancy in common. John Smith would thus have his wife Mary Smith join in a deed with him to: "John Smith and Mary Smith, husband and wife, as joint tenants with full rights of survivorship and not as tenants in common." State laws differ regarding the language needed, but the attorney who draws up any joint-tenancy deed would be aware of the local requirements.

One of the advantages of a joint tenancy is its ease of creation. The other spouse need not even know of its existence in many cases.

When there is a joint tenancy, the surviving joint tenant automatically comes into ownership of the property upon the death of the other tenant or tenants.*

Joint-tenancy property is said to "pass outside the terms of a will" because of this automatic transfer. For this reason joint-tenancy property is considered to be a "nonprobate asset" that passes under the terms of the individual document that creates the joint tenancy rather than under the terms of a will or marriage agreement.

Another reason joint tenancies are often used as the means to avoid PREMAs is that the giver can maintain control of the asset. This is done by the mere expedient of holding on to the certificate, passbook, checkbook, policy, deed, or other asset.

Joint tenancies have often been referred to as "the poor man's will." One of the major arguments against using them more often is the fact that they may cause an increase in death taxes. We will discuss this aspect in Chapter 7, but suffice it now to say that both state and federal laws have recently eased the tax sting of joint tenancies between spouses, especially involving federal estate-tax returns for estates with assets of $600,000 or less.

---

*Death taxes may have to be paid on the property, but the ownership shifts "by operation of law" at the joint tenant's death.

New Purchases in Spouse's Name. Outright gifts and joint tenancies are, as we have seen, relatively easy ways of avoiding restrictive terms of a PREMA when the wealthy party wants to increase his spouse's assets. An even simpler way is to make new purchases in the name of the less wealthy spouse. Over a period of years the couple can make it a point to take title to a large amount of assets in the name of the poorer spouse.

This procedure does not involve the possible pitfalls or legal hassles in transferring existing assets from one party to the other. This way no third parties' (read: children's, relatives', business partners') expectations will be upset. Of course, a disadvantage of this type of program is that it is relatively long-term: you will be waiting for new accumulations in the normal course of things before making the transfers.

Such new purchases may amount to partial or outright gifts, depending upon who furnishes the money. Increasing a spouse's share in this way, though, is a natural, informal, and unobtrusive method of "conspiring" with one's spouse to avoid the provisions of a PREMA without formal amendment.

Insurance. Life insurance is a very effective method of transferring large amounts of money in ways that may be totally contrary to the terms of a PREMA. Providing life insurance benefits to a new spouse—as opposed to, say, the outright gift of the same amount—is much less likely to ruffle the feathers of concerned children of a former marriage. Large premiums may, of course, be prohibitive for older people in many cases, but insurance is a solid option for "informally amending" a PREMA.

Insurance, like joint-tenancy property, is a "nonprobate asset" in the sense that it passes to the beneficiaries stated in the document (here, the insurance policy) rather than to those specified in the will or PREMA. Thus the husband or wife who wishes to increase a spouse's overall share in an estate can simply take out a life insurance policy (usually a less expensive "term" or "universal life" policy) and name the spouse as beneficiary—and possibly owner—of the policy.

While talking about insurance one should note that it is used not only to, in effect, bypass the terms of a PREMA, it is also used quite often in Combination PREMAs to offset transfers or bequests of other assets. In other words, the parties many times agree that the wife, say, will give up her marital rights in return for being named beneficiary in a new life insurance policy the husband takes out on his life.

Trusts. Establishment of a trust is another way a wealthy spouse can treat his partner more generously without tampering with the PREMA. A major advantage of trusts is their tremendous variety and flexibility. Since a trust is a separate legal animal, it, like joint-tenancy property and insurance, transfers and controls assets under its own provisions rather than under the provisions of a will or PREMA. Trusts set up to operate in the here and now are called *inter vivos,* or living, trusts. Those that take effect upon the death of the trustor are referred to as *testamentary* trusts.

Though there is a time and place for everything, including trusts, there are usually easier and quicker ways to get around the terms of a PREMA than resorting to the formation of a trust.

Changing PREMA Provisions by Will. What if, after the PREMA is signed, either party executes a will that has provisions contrary to the PREMA? Is this a valid provision in a will? Does this amend, cancel, or in any way affect the PREMA? This area calls for great caution.

A few general rules. You cannot amend a PREMA by will. A PREMA, as we know, is a contract and as such requires the consent of both parties to effect any change. For this reason it is not possible to execute a will that effectively restricts a spouse to less than he or she would have received under the existing PREMA. It is possible, though, to be more generous to a spouse in a will than the PREMA provides for.*

*This assumes, of course, that rights of third parties have not intervened. For example, property that has been sold, encumbered, or contracted for

57

Done properly, a will can be a workable adjunct to a PREMA, but a will or codicil that is flubbed can have disastrous effects. Attempting to change a PREMA by a will lays it open to the interpretation that it has been superseded or terminated entirely. A surviving spouse might argue that substance should control over mere form and that, after all, when the (now-deceased) spouse signed a will with provisions contrary to the PREMA, it was really his intention to cancel the PREMA. The decedent, of course, would be at rather a disadvantage in expressing himself upon the subject.

Even if a PREMA survives any attempt to amend it by will, there is a danger that arises from the other side—the danger that the will provision will not be given *any effect at all.* Unhappy children of a former marriage might take the position that (1) any will provision that is contrary to the PREMA is void because the PREMA language controls, and (2) the surviving spouse has specifically relinquished, by virtue of the PREMA language, all claim to the decedent's estate except as provided in the PREMA. This latter argument is sometimes advanced even though no attempt is made in the will to amend the PREMA, the point being made that a surviving spouse cannot at the same time admit the validity of the PREMA and also make a claim to an estate in which she has supposedly given up all rights.

Sometimes the beneficiaries under an amended will more generous to the spouse than the PREMA allege that the testator lacked testamentary capacity when he signed it. The very inconsistency between the two documents, they claim, is proof positive of mental incapacity. Ol' Dad would never have done this if he had been in his right mind. After all, why would he go to all the trouble to draw up a premarital agreement and then in effect destroy it by a later will?

Other questions automatically arise in the course of such internecine battles. Will contestants can argue that the execu-

---

transfer to another cannot be given to a spouse so as to deprive third parties of their rightful claims.

tor has the fiduciary duty to uphold the provisions of the PREMA, while the surviving spouse can counter that the executor must abide by the terms of the will. Conflict-of-interest charges run rampant in such situations.

In view of the above problems, should people just forget about ever executing a will or codicil that gives a spouse more than the PREMA allows? No, but at least a couple of precautions should be taken:

1. The will or codicil should acknowledge the existence of the PREMA and should state that it is not an attempted amendment of the PREMA.*
2. The PREMA should contain language that anticipates and authorizes possible will provisions which could be more generous than the PREMA. What you want to say, in effect, is that a spouse's waivers and relinquishment of rights in the PREMA shall not prohibit him or her from also taking under the terms of the spouse's will. (The PREMA forms in Appendix 1 of this book contain the necessary language regarding this important element.)

All Give More. Each of the foregoing methods, then, is a way to change the effect of a PREMA after it is signed. Each obviously involves some manner of giving *more* to a spouse. Most of the methods do not even require the consent of the other party. Of course as we have discussed earlier in the book, any attempt to give a spouse *less* than a PREMA requires might well be fraudulent, unless done with his or her consent, supported by sufficient consideration.

The Question of Secrecy. The reasons people desire secrecy are many, and not necessarily the most laudatory. But what-

---

*Example: "I hereby bequeath to my wife Mary Jane Smith the sum of $50,000. This bequest is in addition to the sum(s), if any, which she would have received under one certain Premarital Agreement entered into between my said wife and me on June 1, 1987. Nothing herein is intended to amend or terminate said Agreement, which at this time remains in full force and effect."

ever the rationale, a good question often arises: What is the best way to keep any changes confidential? Let's assume that husband Charlie wants to give more to wife Edith than his PREMA provides. He does not want to have to explain his actions to his children, his in-laws, his banker, and his next-door neighbor. He wants things simple and quiet, and that's that.

How do the methods that we have discussed of changing a PREMA weigh in on the confidentiality scale?

Joint tenancies in financial accounts are simple and quick and relatively private. In almost all cases not even the spouse need know of the existence of the joint tenancy (though his or her social security number may be required on certain documents). It's an extremely easy thing for Charlie to add Edith's name to a certificate of deposit or savings account. Nothing is recorded at the courthouse, and no "official" records can be searched through by anyone who wants to know your business.

Secrecy can also usually be maintained by the simple expedient of outright purchase of stock or securities in the name of the other spouse. Remember, however, that if the assets transferred are income-producing, the spouse will probably receive end-of-year 1099s disclosing the amount of interest or dividends paid during the year. (In most instances, of course, one would *want* the spouse to be aware of a change in his or her favor—but that is begging the question of secrecy.)

If secrecy is a consideration, one should not overlook the more obvious transfers of *things*, such as cash or jewelry. These transfers can be just as confidential as the parties want to keep them.

Insurance is more complicated than either the creation of a joint tenancy or a gift, but secrecy can be maintained with most types of life insurance. What I am discussing here is insurance on the life of the giver. It is almost impossible to obtain insurance on the life of adult insureds without their knowledge, if for no other reason than the physical examination requirement.

A deed of real estate is usually recorded at the local court-house.* So much for confidentiality.

If Charlie wants to enter into an Amendment or a Termina-tion Agreement, Edith will obviously have to know about it because she will have to sign the document. Again, Charlie will in practically all instances want Edith to know what he is doing. If the two of them live in a state that requires record-ing,† and if they absolutely demand secrecy, then their best bet for confidential transfers would be through the joint-tenancy, outright gift, or insurance methods.

One last point about changing or terminating a PREMA, or giving additional property to a spouse after the marriage. Don't promise that you are going to do these things at the time the original document is signed. Of course all future possibili-ties and options can be discussed, but as soon as you promise to do something in the future you have the obligation to do it and might well be forced to do it by the court. Even though every PREMA should contain the standard language prohibit ing oral modifications and asserting the document contains the full agreement of the parties, you should not start out with a misstatement of fact.

What if such oral promise is made and not abided by? When called to testify at some future time, can the promising party hide behind the prohibition against oral modifications and deny under oath that he made such an oral inducement? Hardly. So it's a dilemma to be avoided.

---

*Not recording a deed until after the death of the giver may cause real problems regarding whether or not there was ever an intention to legally "deliver" the deed. In most cases *where a PREMA exists* I would advise against the practice of holding a deed without recording it.

†Recording would rarely be necessary for validity of a PREMA *as between the parties.*

61

6. Do You Need a Lawyer?

"He saw a lawyer killing a viper
On a dunghill hard by his stable
And the Devil smiled,
For it put him in mind
Of Cain and his brother Abel."

—Samuel Taylor Coleridge,
"The Devil's Thoughts"

It would be fun to say that this book answers all the questions about PREMAs; that you need not look outside its covers; and that a lawyer is not needed. There would be a kind of perverse glee trying to duck the arrows of outrageous fortune flung my way by fellow attorneys.

In point of fact, it may well be that a good number of people reading this book actually *can* prepare an effective PREMA using this book alone and without additional advice from a lawyer. There are several reasons for this. The first is that many lawyers have never written a PREMA and are quite ignorant upon the subject. Lawyers in general practice brush up against premarital agreement–related questions only on rare occasions, and even in large firms you will not find someone specializing exclusively in premarital agreements (not that you would necessarily want to go to such a narrowly specialized person in any event). Even among bank trust departments there is a dearth of information on this subject.*

There is a second, if somewhat imperfect, beginning rule for gauging the need for a lawyer: If you have nothing but debts (or very few assets) and the PREMA is kept uncomplicated, your need for a lawyer diminishes accordingly.

Third, many people go to lawyers for the wrong reasons anyway. I have seen people walk into a lawyer's office, hat in hand, and ask him what would be the proper thing to do with their property. Making that kind of decision is not the lawyer's business. You should establish your own goals and have at least a general idea how you would like to achieve them. Let the lawyer explain the mechanics of accomplishing your goals and inform you if your proposals have failed to comply with local state law in some respect. But don't let him, or expect him to, tell you what your mind is about your own property.

The foregoing having been said, however, there are at least two reasons why you may want to, or in some cases must, have an attorney involved.

The Attorney's Stomping Ground. There are various specialized areas of law and taxes in which you may well need to consult an attorney and/or a certified public accountant. Oftentimes your goals can be achieved by taking several radically different legal routes, and the advice of a specialist can be very important. Examples: Achieving your goals may involve transactions with family corporate stock, or corporate liquidations, or establishment of trusts or mergers. Documents such as deeds, mortgages, bills of sale, assignments, articles of incorporation, bylaws, partnership agreements, and wills are all on the lawyer's stomping ground. So let him stomp.

Though it is possible to prepare legal documents without an

*Before writing this book I checked with the trust departments of the banks in town and, although there was of course extensive information about wills and trusts, there was nothing usable to be found about marriage contracts in general and premarital, or antenuptial, agreements in particular.

attorney, it is often foolish to do so, especially when substantial values are involved. In the long run you will not save anything financially by skimping in this area. It's the old penny-wise pound-foolish maxim.

The real point, though, is this: The preparation of such documents concerns the *mechanics* of putting your PREMA into effect. Leave that to the lawyer, either now or after you die, depending on the thrust of your plans. But do not allow yourselves to be reduced to some boiler-plated form with the same financial life (or death) plan that almost everyone else in the world has. You're the boss. If after reading this book you have some very definite ideas about setting up a premarital agreement, do not give up on them unless there are some good legal reasons for it.

Only you and your spouse-to-be thoroughly know what your hopes and plans are. If you have in fact managed to accumulate some wealth over the years, you will probably not be a complete stranger to attorneys. So, don't lose heart if you must talk to a local lawyer under the guidelines I will explain. Later in this chapter I will offer some suggestions about the best way to utilize the skills of an attorney.

The Advantage of Independent Legal Counsel. In certain cases it is not so important *what* the attorney says as *who* says it. In other words, if your prospective spouse consults his or her own attorney before signing a PREMA, the very fact that independent legal counsel was involved is (almost) worth its weight in gold. Stated a third way: The fact that two attorneys reviewed the document before it was signed might be the best insurance policy you can buy in upholding the document against later attack under the various grounds mentioned in Chapter 3.

Don't worry about the possibility that the "other side" will consult an attorney on matters pertaining to a PREMA. Only two things can happen. Your future spouse's attorney will advise the spouse to sign the PREMA (possibly with changes) or he'll advise against signing it. If he acquiesces in the document, you have, as we mentioned, bought yourself a tremendous amount of protection against future attack based upon allegations of coercion, fraud, mistake, or misrepresentation. If, on the other hand, the attorney feels the document is defective or unfair in some way, you might as well know about it right *now* rather than later.

In future years, more and more states will probably be virtually *requiring* that the two signing parties have independent legal counsel. On January 1, 1985, for example, a California law became effective which in effect prohibited the enforcement of restrictive PREMA provisions against a spouse who "was not represented by independent legal counsel at the time of signing of the agreement."*

Case law and the general statutory trend throughout the states are leaning ever more toward favoring independent legal counsel.

Taking everything into consideration, I believe that most people will opt to, and should, see a local lawyer before signing their PREMA. In some cases, the PREMA could, after all, be the most wide-ranging legal document they will ever sign.

When to Get the Attorney Involved.   My suggestion is that you prepare your PREMA in full, using the forms or combination of forms in Appendix 1 of this book. Only then, after you have prepared the document as you want it, should you go to the attorney's office for a review of your plan. Even this office visit may not be necessary in some instances in respect to, say, a Prior Property PREMA with few complications.

In going to the lawyer, keep in mind your purpose for being there. Use his knowledge to ensure that your PREMA will pass muster under the most recent decisions of your highest state court and the most recent enactments of your state legislature.† Most of your questions should be specific: Have there been any recent changes in state law that will affect my

---

*California Probate Code, Sections 140–47. These sections have in turn been superseded by California's adoption of the substance of the Uniform Premarital Agreement Act.

†Though the state law of every jurisdiction has been examined in preparing this book, the statutory and case law is constantly evolving.

PREMA? Should my PREMA be recorded? Are community property rights involved? Should I split any joint tenancies or should I enter into any; and if so, exactly how is a joint tenancy with right of survivorship created in my state? Should I change my ownership or beneficiary designations of my life insurance policies in any way? How exposed am I to federal estate or state inheritance taxes? Does the lawyer see any future problems in the area of full disclosure, undue influence, or misrepresentation? Is my divorce contingency provision (if I use one) acceptable?

Asking such specific questions of your attorney will put him on notice that you are already well founded in your basic PREMA plan. Don't let your questions wander all over the realm of civil law. I recommend that you have your questions listed in advance and, as you go through them, jot down answers in spaces after each one. Don't be turned off by the lawyer who admits that he is not sure of an answer and wants to check into the matter further. Such an honest response is much better than a shoot-from-the-hip answer from an attorney who feels that he must give an immediate and definite response on a topic simply because a question has been asked.

Attorney Fees. How do you raise the question of attorney fees? As soon as you dispose of the usual pleasantries about the weather, you should lose no time asking the attorney about his fees. He will not be insulted (if he is, you're in the wrong place), and you will both feel better about the matter once the fee arrangement is determined.

Once the attorney is aware that you are well informed about PREMAs, things will run much more smoothly, even in the area of the fee. Of course you must take care not to simply roll over and let the attorney take your proposed PREMA, retype it with a few superficial changes, and then charge you in the same manner as if he had created the thing from nothing for you. Such a legal practice would be a bit like the attorney who, instead of using a perfectly good preprinted bar association legal form, has his secretary type out the document verbatim.

The result is a complicated-looking seven-page typewritten document costing several hundred dollars instead of a one-sheet form with a price tag one-fourth that.

Attorney fees usually range anywhere from about fifty dollars an hour on the low end to more than one hundred dollars an hour on the upper end. Time spent reviewing the document should be in the half-hour to hour range for most people, though complications and additional work (which might not necessarily be required by the PREMA alone) could increase the time. If the attorney is going to be doing something for you other than a review of your PREMA, ask specifically what it will be. Consultations with your fiancé's (or fiancée's) counsel may be necessary. Many times the attorney will agree that his charge will be no more than a stated amount unless he tells you otherwise. This is a very workable way to keep an attorney's fee well within limits. If the attorney insists on a completely open-ended fee arrangement, go elsewhere. Such a person may know nothing about marriage contracts and simply want you to pay him to educate himself entirely on the subject.

Obviously, if your attorney and your prospective spouse's attorney have been intensely negotiating a few points, your fee will rise accordingly.

Who Types Up the Final PREMA Document? Unless you have agreed to major changes in the substance of the PREMA that you and your future spouse have presented to the lawyer(s), it is certainly not necessary to have the lawyer's secretary retype it for you. Of course, much depends on the lawyer's involvement. If two sets of attorneys have gone at the language hammer and tongs, it would obviously be inappropriate for you to insist on typing the final agreed-upon draft yourself. But if contact with the attorneys has been minimal and your proposed document has been reviewed and is approved by all, there is no good reason for you not to finish the job you and your spouse-to-be have so ably started. It's also cheaper that way.

The Advantage of an Intermediary. Sometimes certain points have to be made to the other side that a party would rather take poison than bring up himself. He or she feels something would be lost in the relationship if it were necessary to personally argue a sensitive item in a PREMA on through to settlement. There is an undeniable appeal about two people going out to dinner while the lawyers make their debating points and get the document in final form. If there is a matter one of you absolutely can't force yourself to delve into when it must be delved into, then your lawyer is the one to do it.

Two parting points. Someone once said that "the law protects everybody who can afford to hire a good lawyer." But remember this: a good civil-trial lawyer or real estate lawyer or corporation lawyer or criminal lawyer or divorce lawyer may not know a thing about premarital agreements. So you surely need not go to a "big-name" lawyer for help. After reading this book you will know, after only a few minutes' discussion, whether the lawyer you're talking to is knowledgeable in this area. Legal knowledge and willingness to get the job done right are much more important than a lawyer's fame in unrelated areas of law.

Lastly, some people are not only unconcerned about high legal fees but they actually seek out high chargers based on a you-get-what-you-pay-for philosophy. Wrong. The most expensive foods might kill you, the highest-priced dress might look terrible on you (even if you're a woman), high-priced art can be junk, high-cost health care treatments might be dangerous quackery. So, keep both feet on the ground and don't look for legal gimmicks at exotic prices.

7. PREMAs and Taxes

"And the tax collectors of Pharaoh spread like lice throughout the land."

—H. Life

If you write the definitive book on, say, the anatomy of the human hand, the internal combustion engine, or Impressionist art, you will not be very successful trying to write and sell a new book on the very same subject the next year. Not so with taxes. Tens of thousands of people make a living based on the fact that our tax laws are constantly changing. It is not even possible, in fact, to write a book about taxes that will be completely authoritative for just one year. It is for this reason that publishers of tax services must print their volumes on loose-leaf paper, so that things can be updated on a weekly basis throughout the year.

All of which is to say that I am not going to attempt here to set forth the substantive laws of taxation. After the close of your tax year (usually December 31 for individual taxpayers) you and your tax preparer can face up to your income tax return based upon the most up-to-the-minute tax law. What we shall do in this chapter, then, is outline the relationship between PREMAs and taxes based on present tax laws.

Filing Federal Income Tax Returns. The Internal Revenue Code allows, if you will, a loophole for people who have signed a PREMA. Even though you and your spouse have entered into a PREMA—thereby giving up ownership in, or any claim to ownership in, certain income-producing assets of the other party—the federal government still allows you to have the advantages of filing a *joint* federal income tax return each year.

In the past there has almost always been a tax benefit in filing a joint, as opposed to separate, federal income tax return for married people. This was true at practically every level of income. It was noted, for example, when vice-presidential candidate Geraldine Ferraro disclosed the income tax returns she and her husband had filed prior to the 1984 elections, that she had elected to file separate income tax returns for various years. Tax analysts were quick to point out that, although she may well have had some non-tax reason for filing a separate federal return, she definitely paid more income tax than would have been necessary had she filed a joint return with her husband.

With the decrease in tax bracket categories brought about by the tax revisions made by Congress in 1986, the benefits of filing jointly will be greatly reduced for most people, but not all. Your individual income tax adviser should see which filing status works out better for you.

Even though in logic one might argue that spouses should not be able to file joint tax returns if certain PREMAs are in effect—because the income is separate, not joint—existing law nonetheless allows such joint filing. The great majority of husbands and wives who have signed PREMAs should take full advantage of this leniency in the federal law unless there are good non-tax reasons for filing separately and paying more money.

Filing State Income Tax Returns. States have their own systems of income taxation. Many states allow you and your spouse to elect to file separate state income tax returns without "penalty" even though the two of you have filed joint federal income tax returns. Contrary to the rule of thumb at the federal level, it is often an advantage to file separately on state tax returns.

My advice regarding filing status on state returns is basic: If your state allows you to elect whether to file jointly or separately, it will *probably* be beneficial to you to file separately at the state level *if* your state has a graduated income tax rate. The reason for this is that instead of having to add, say, the wife's income on top of the husband's already high-rate bracket—with the result that it will be taxed at a higher overall rate than the husband's—the wife can begin at the lowest rate in the book with her separate income.* Of course if that same wife has no income of her own, or if the state has a flat income tax rate (or one that is based on a percentage of federal income tax), there would be no savings of state tax by filing separately.

Where parties file separately on the state level, a PREMA can sometimes give an incidental benefit. Sometimes a state tax audit revolves only around proving whose income is whose when separate income tax returns are filed. In such cases a PREMA provides a perfect and undeniable proof for the allocation of income between the spouses.

Federal Estate Tax. In the last decade there have been profound changes in federal estate-tax law. The two greatest changes involve the "unlimited marital deduction" and the "unified tax credit." Because of these two changes alone the number of estates now within the taxable category has decreased to only about 3 percent of all estates at the federal level.

Some of you may remember that just a few years ago the federal estate-tax law allowed only about one half of a spouse's estate to pass tax-free to the survivor. The result was

---

*For example, assume the state tax rate starts at the zero bracket and ends at the 15 percent bracket. It makes much more sense to have each spouse start at the zero bracket and work up to about 10 percent than to have one spouse start at zero and the other spouse start at 10 percent and then work up toward the maximum 15 percent.

a great variety of "marital deduction trusts" which were set up to take advantage of the maximum amount that could be given to a spouse without payment of taxes. Now, however, *all* qualifying transfers to a survivor upon the death of the first to die pass tax-free! A transfer to a spouse is, then, a tax shelter so long as the second spouse lives.

People with large estates should be aware of this tax "goodie" they are passing up if they give little or nothing to their spouse by way of a PREMA. There are sometimes, of course, offsetting non-tax reasons for restrictive PREMAs, as we have discussed earlier in the book, but people contemplating a PREMA who have estates of about $600,000 should at least consider this lost federal tax benefit.

With this relatively new unlimited marital deduction (no longer restricted to the old maximum of one-half the estate), then, a spouse can at death transfer to the other spouse $5,000 or $50 million and the result is the same: no federal estate tax at the transferor's death.

But we had better control our enthusiasm. What the government giveth with the unlimited marital deduction it also taketh away, at least partially. A trap lies behind the kindly smile of the tax man. What people sometimes overlook is that when the second spouse dies there is no spouse left to take advantage of the marital deduction. It is then that the government gets its pound of flesh. Therefore, in large estates when the full unlimited marital deduction is used at the death of the first spouse, some of the federal estate tax has often only been *delayed* rather than avoided.

The result is that after the first rush of euphoria about the unlimited marital deduction law, people have been much more cautious in abandoning their old trusts. It is now generally recognized that if the total estate of the husband and wife is less than about $600,000, the entire estate can be willed to a spouse, and a marital deduction trust is not a necessity *for tax reasons only.* * Current strategy is to try to make outright

---

*Trusts might still be necessary for non-estate-tax reasons such as professional management of trust assets, retention of some control over assets, or a desire to "generation-skip" in the transfer of assets.

transfers to the spouse (thereby taking full advantage of the marital deduction) in smaller estates, and to use a combination of marital deduction, unified credit, and trusts in larger estates.

All things considered, the effect of the unlimited marital deduction in estate planning has been massive.

We have talked about the consequences of the unlimited marital deduction, but what of the second half of the new dynamic duo of federal estate-tax reduction, the unified credit? Exactly what is it and how can it affect, or be affected by, a PREMA?

Beginning in 1981 a different concept was introduced into federal estate-tax law. Whereas in prior years each estate was allowed to exclude from tax consideration a certain amount of assets ($60,000, for example) before the adding and subtracting began in arriving at the net taxable estate, in 1981 this exclusion or exemption was done away with entirely. Instead, the law provided for a *credit* against the tax as finally calculated. People immediately saw that this credit translated into an estate of a given size. For example, a unified credit of $47,000 translated into a nontaxable estate of $175,625.

The total unified credit provided for in the tax law was programmed to be implemented in steps over a period of seven years. The years, the unified credit, and the equivalent size of the nontaxable estate are as set out below.

From the chart below it is plain to see why we have previously talked about estates with reference to whether they were above or below $600,000. The practical effect of the unified credit is that in 1987 all estates with taxable assets

Year	Unified Credit	Size of Nontaxable Estate
1981	$47,000	$175,625
1982	$62,800	$225,000
1983	$79,300	$275,000
1984	$96,300	$325,000
1985	$121,800	$400,000
1986	$155,800	$500,000
1987 on	$192,800	$600,000

of $600,000 or less will escape all federal taxes.*

With proper planning a couple can pass along an estate of at least $1.2 million simply by using a combination of the marital deduction and the unified credit. One rather simple way to accomplish this would be to transfer one half of the estate ($600,000) to the surviving spouse outright, and the other half ($600,000) to a trust. The trust could provide income to the surviving spouse for life, with the trust balance passing to the children (or others) upon the death of the surviving spouse.

The mathematics in such a scheme are not complicated: The $600,000 passing outright to the surviving spouse goes tax-free because of the marital deduction. The other $600,000 that goes into a trust for the benefit of the spouse does *not* pass tax-free under the marital deduction rules because title does not vest in the spouse, nor does she have the power to control the property. The second $600,000 *does* pass tax-free, though, because of the unified credit. So the full $1.2 million passes tax-free when the husband dies, half shielded by the marital deduction and half shielded by the unified credit. Then, when the wife dies, no tax is payable again because the wife owns only (I feel guilty using "only" when talking about this kind of money) $600,000, and the unified credit wipes out the tax on this amount.

Such results with such a simple estate plan were impossible just a few years ago.

I have referred to the federal estate-tax law in only the broadest terms solely to show the general concepts we are dealing with. As I mentioned in Chapter 6, there are certain areas properly called the lawyer's stomping grounds. Drafting wills that incorporate estate plans such as we discussed above are just such stomping grounds. Even at that, you should, after

---

*We must speak generally here. For example, large gifts made during the life of the decedent will decrease the size of the unified credit. Also, a taxable estate of $600,000 might have begun much larger than that, but because of the use of various deductions such as for charitable bequests, death and burial expenses, taxes, administration costs, and the marital deduction, the estate was reduced to that figure.

learning the dos and don'ts from your lawyer, try to put into effect an estate plan as close to your *own* as possible within the framework of those dos and don'ts.

Every lawyer in general practice draws up dozens—usually hundreds—of wills during the course of his practice. During those same years that lawyer will often have drawn up no PREMAs at all. It is mainly for that reason that I have no hesitation advising you after reading this book to carry the ball as much as possible with your PREMA but to hand off the ball to the lawyer regarding your will preparation and execution.

PREMAs and Federal Estate Taxes. As we have said before, after 1986 you do not have to worry about federal estate tax if your estate will not exceed $600,000, because the unified credit will cancel any taxes owing on estates smaller than that. However, let us assume for the purposes of this discussion that at the time of your death your estate will be larger than that amount. Let us further assume that you are going to enter into a PREMA and then marry.

There are some tax traps lying in wait for the innocent. The first is that not every kind of devise* to a surviving spouse qualifies as a tax-free marital deduction transfer. So you should make sure that *whatever you devise to your spouse qualifies for the marital deduction.* Why pay substantial taxes because of a mistake in the form of a death transfer to a spouse?

The magic bureaucratic tax phrase in this area is "qualified terminable interest" (I hated to say it, but I had to). If a devise to a surviving spouse is a "qualifying terminable interest," the transfer will qualify for the marital deduction and be considered tax-free. That's good. If the devise is considered merely a "terminable interest," the marital deduction is lost for that asset. That's bad, because it's taxable.

The distinction is based mostly upon whether or not the devise results in a transfer of the entire interest in the property

---

*Though "devise" historically just referred to a transfer of *real estate* at death, and "bequest" to a transfer of *personal property,* most modern probate codes use "devise" in connection with any type of property transferred by will. I use it in this all-inclusive sense.

to the surviving spouse. If the entire interest passes, it is usually considered a qualifying terminable interest (the good kind); and if the devise results in something less than the entire interest passing to the spouse, the tax man moves in for the kill.

Here are two examples.

First, a husband and wife signed a Combination PREMA under the terms of which the wife would be given a life estate* in the valuable home of the husband. The "present value" of the life estate at the time of the death of the husband is $40,000. The present value of such a life estate would probably *not* qualify for the marital deduction because the right to live in the home has strings attached—after the wife's death the home transfers to others or their heirs or assigns. In other words, a life estate in such a residential property would probably be considered only a "terminable interest," not a qualified terminable interest.

Second, as part of a PREMA the wife agrees to set up a trust which, at her death, provides for payment of $1,000 a month during the life of the husband. Does the present value of the monthly payments from the trust for the life of the husband qualify for the marital deduction as a qualifying terminable interest? Again, probably not. The Internal Revenue Code requires that when less than the entire interest in a property is transferred, *all* the following conditions be met in order for the marital deduction to be taken:

1. The asset must pass from the deceased to the surviving spouse either by life estate or in trust;
2. The transfer document must provide that *all* of the income from the asset must go to the surviving spouse, and the income must be payable annually or at more frequent intervals.
3. The surviving spouse must have the power of appointment;†

---

*A life estate in land refers in this case to the right to have, occupy, and use the home so long as the wife should live. A life estate is not assignable or transferable by the life tenant (the wife, here), either while alive or by will.

†"Power of appointment" as used here refers to the right of the surviving spouse to transfer or assign the property to himself or herself while alive,

4. The power of appointment must belong to the surviving spouse alone, without limitation;
5. Nobody other than the surviving spouse may have the power of appointment to anyone other than the surviving spouse.

It is clear that both the foregoing examples would not qualify for the marital deduction because of lack of compliance with the power of appointment conditions. Because of this, both PREMA provisions would be considered to grant terminable interests, and therefore the assets transferred would be taxable, even though the assets were used by, or the payments went to, the surviving spouse. But don't forget that even though the transfer does not qualify for the marital deduction and is consequently "taxable," it may still escape taxation if the estate is under $600,000, because of the unified credit. As I have mentioned, much of this discussion is moot if the estate with which you are concerned is below the $600,000 level.

In summary, those who are contemplating using a restrictive PREMA should be aware that it may result in the payment of more federal estate taxes in larger estates.* In other estates it may simply result in the payment of taxes sooner than otherwise.

If both spouses have large estates in their own right, the marital deduction loses some of its benefit, because a transfer of assets to an already wealthy husband or wife simply creates tax problems at the death of the later to die. All these things will be discussed in detail with you by your tax planner if you are fortunate enough to fit within the estate brackets we are talking about.

For most people a $600,000 estate will never be attained. As we have observed before, only about 3 percent of the population will ever have to worry about paying federal taxes under the new rules. But before you get too smug about your situation don't forget that life insurance *is* considered a taxable asset for federal purposes. Such life insurance, whether pur-

---

or to specify in such spouse's will who shall receive it at his or her death.

*"Larger estates" in connection with federal estate tax refers to those in excess of a taxable amount of $600,000.

chased personally or through an employer, sometimes unexpectedly throws people into the taxable category, especially if double indemnity provisions kick in, such as when accidental death occurs.

Federal Gift Tax. Gift taxes are assessed in respect to transfers without adequate consideration. That having been said, though, it must quickly be added that in the future very few people will have to pay any federal gift tax. There are several reasons for this. First, there is now an annual exclusion of $10,000 per donee (recipient) per year, and $20,000 per donee per year if a spouse joins in the gifts. In other words, a husband and wife with three children could jointly give $20,000 per child per year—$60,000 each year—without incurring any tax liability. Second, if the donee is a spouse, there is now an unlimited amount that can be transferred without incurring tax liability (similar to the unlimited marital deduction for federal estate-tax purposes). Third, even if gift tax would otherwise be payable, the unified credit will cancel any tax owing for taxable gifts up to $600,000 in 1987 and after. Any credit used to offset gift tax liability, though, will be subtracted from the amount available to offset federal estate tax at death.

The amount of unified credit available to offset gift tax liability is the same as the credit shown in the chart in the discussion about federal estate tax on page 73.

A couple entering into a PREMA should rarely if ever have to be concerned with payment of federal gift taxes in regard to transfers between themselves. After all, (1) a transfer *before* marriage pursuant to a PREMA is not a "gift," but rather in fulfillment of a binding contract, and (2) if the transfer between the couple is made *after* the marriage, the unlimited marital exclusion for gifts between spouses would apply in any event.

State Death Taxes. Almost all states levy some form of death tax.* State taxes are usually *inheritance,* as opposed to estate,

---

*Florida's weather is not the only reason that wealthy older people choose to retire there. Florida imposes no state death taxes.

taxes. One of the main differences between the two types of death taxes is that whereas the estate tax is assessed against the estate itself, inheritance taxes are assessed against the individual receiving the particular share of the estate. Because of a myriad of exclusions, exemptions, and rate differences, two people who were devised the same amount under a will often find that the size of their net after-tax devise differs quite a bit.

There are a couple of practical differences between federal estate and state inheritance taxes: (1) Because of the new federal tax rules, the payment of federal estate taxes is limited to only the largest estates, involving relatively few people. Many more people end up paying state inheritance taxes. (2) Though state inheritance taxes are imposed much more often than federal estate taxes, the rates are usually much, much lower. For example, state rates often start at 1 or 2 percent and range up to a maximum of about 15 percent or so for the very largest devises. Federal rates usually kick in, after the unified credit is used, at about 35 percent and range up to a maximum after 1985 of 50 percent for taxable estates over $2.5 million.*

The final question we must ask then, as regarding all taxes, is: How much of a consideration should state death taxes be if a PREMA is being contemplated? Almost none. I cannot imagine that a PREMA would or would not be executed solely because of state inheritance tax considerations. True, more taxes might have to be paid if a spouse is excluded from receiving his or her normal statutory share, but the amount will *usually* be relatively small and would scarcely ever tip the scales one way or the other. The payment, on the other hand, of additional federal estate taxes because of a restrictive PREMA would be a greater factor in deciding against signing a PREMA for tax reasons alone. Once past the federal estate-tax hurdle in your considerations, the state death-tax ramifications will pretty much fall in line.

Remember, we are talking about fairly large estates here,

---

*As recently as 1983 the top rate was 60 percent, which was applied to estates over $3.5 million.

and in my opinion the "life" considerations should be much more important than the comparatively small amount of state death taxes that hang in the balance. If, for example, someone with a half-million-dollar estate has good reasons to otherwise enter into a PREMA, but then retreats from doing so because heirs might someday have to pay 5 percent more in taxes, maybe that someone's priorities are mixed up. The tax tail is being allowed to wag the dog. Add 35 percent or so federal estate taxes into the equation and you have a real element to consider. But, back out of a PREMA because of state death taxes alone? No.

The last paragraph brings up a point that is too often glossed over in estate planning. In an attempt to show clients how they can save a *relatively* small amount of money, attorneys, CPAs, and trust officers sometimes force their clients and customers to go through all kinds of legal contortions that are most unnatural for people in their waning years. I say "force" because people are sometimes made to believe that they are coldhearted and uncaring if they do not live their last years according to a formula whose sole rationale is to save as much money as possible for other people. The weird result in the United States is that at a time when old people should be enjoying the fruits of many years of hard work and scrimping and saving, they are told to give their money away, put it in trust, or relinquish control of it. They go on a dole to their children or trust officer. The natural confidence and respect that control of their own destiny should engender is lost and not even discussed.

Of course taxes should be a concern for all of us. But a happy medium (I guess "happy" can never be properly used in relation to taxes) must be struck. Don't let tax planning rule your lives. *Do not* give your property away just to "make yourself poor" in order to save somebody some death taxes when you are gone. Many people have been prevailed upon to do just that, and many people have been made very unhappy because of it.

8. Other Agreements

There are other agreements and there are Other Agreements. Some are definitely enforceable, some are not, and it is impossible to predict what a court would do with the rest.

Postmarital Agreements (POSTMAs). This book thus far has been devoted almost entirely to *pre*marital agreements. I have pointed out how dangerous it is to attempt to take away a spouse's rights by an agreement signed after the marriage (a POSTMA).

What if, however, two spouses wish to enter into a marriage agreement after their marriage? Is there any way at all this can be done validly?

The answer is yes, but the obstacles are greater, especially if substantial marital rights are given up by one of the spouses. The first thing to keep in mind is that all of the rules regarding disclosure of assets, coercion, undue influence, fraud, and misrepresentation which apply to PREMAs apply with equal force to POSTMAs. So a document that has been signed because of, say, a man's fraud after the marriage is just as vulner-

81

able to attack as the document signed because of his fraud before the marriage. In fact, because of the confidential relationship that exists between a husband and wife, any agreement between them will often be subjected to much greater scrutiny by the courts than otherwise. The biggest difficulty with POSTMAs, though, is their lack of legal consideration when a spouse gives something up without receiving something worthwhile in return.

The consideration cannot be, for example, to pay for the necessities of life for the spouse, to perform household chores, to have sex with the spouse, or to do any number of things normally done in a husband-wife relationship. These things are considered part and parcel of marriage, and no additional value can be accorded to them in the legal sense.

The Model Probate Code, which has been adopted in many states, in whole or in part, provides that the right of a surviving spouse to take against the will of the deceased spouse "may be waived before *or after* marriage by written contract, agreement or waiver, signed by the party waiving the right, providing the thing or promise given such party is a fair consideration under all the circumstances. The promise of marriage, in the absence of fraud, shall be a sufficient consideration in the case of an agreement made before marriage" (emphasis added).

The Model Probate Code, then, agrees with our earlier discussions to the effect that the mere promise to marry is considered sufficient consideration for a PREMA. But the cases throughout the states show that a POSTMA is much more apt to be stricken down for one or another of the reasons discussed in Chapter 2.

What if a person wants to give *more* to the spouse than the one third or one half otherwise required in the particular jurisdiction? Is legal consideration needed? No. Although in a very few cases a POSTMA with these provisions may be appropriate, in most cases this will be accomplished by outright transfers or by provisions in a last will and testament.

It has been my experience that POSTMAs are of most value

when the husband and wife are agreeing to the manner of division of assets upon the death of one of them. In other words, rather than try to drastically limit one of the parties, the agreement spells out methods of transfer, or particular types, of assets that will pass at death. This is often extremely important in maintaining control in a family business or keeping a long-held family home or other asset intact.

Nonfinancial Agreements. Nowadays a couple will sometimes enter into an agreement that states what each hopes to accomplish in the marriage, what the general duties of each shall be, what each expects of the other, how children will be treated, how free time will be spent, and many other personal matters. In fact, some premarriage counselors encourage such written expressions of hopes and plans in an effort to have the parties determine if they will be traveling down the same marital road after the ceremony. All well and good.

But do not look to the courts to enforce these agreements. They're just not enforceable. If Walter has promised Mary that he will faithfully do half the housework, get up with the babies at night half the time, stop his drinking, never try to move the family more than fifty miles from Mary's hometown, and never talk to his old girlfriend Betty again, Mary has a list of promises and that's it.

Agreements to raise a child in a particular religion are exceptions in some states to the general rule regarding unenforceability of such "intimate" contracts. Some have been upheld and some not.

Living-Together Agreements. In years gone by the courts often refused to enforce an agreement that directly or indirectly condoned adultery, fornication, or other activity contrary to the criminal laws of the court's jurisdiction. Recently, though, the codes of many states have decriminalized adultery, for example, under the "consenting adult" philosophy of modern criminal law. There is very little case law on the subject.

83

The celebrated cases involving actor Lee Marvin* and tennis star Billie Jean King† made many people aware of the dangers of living-together arrangements, whether opposite-sex or same-sex. People have come to believe that it might be best to put down in writing just what should happen financially in the event of a breakup of the relationship. Will an agreement entered into between two such parties be upheld by a court? The answer has to be: It may well be upheld, and in any event such agreement is vastly better than nothing.

If you will recall, I mentioned in an earlier chapter that one of the reasons the courts hesitate to enforce a PREMA with a provision that it shall take effect in the event of a divorce between the parties is that such a document might be construed to encourage divorce. Anything that encourages divorce or promotes instability of the family is considered contrary to public policy. But such rationale would not apply to living-together arrangements. The courts might, then, be more willing to enforce such agreements. On the other hand, I can envision some judges taking the view that the enforcement of living-together agreements would, in itself, possibly encourage relationships contrary to the generally held values of society.

The best approach, then, is probably this: *If* two people are determined to go ahead with such an arrangement, it only makes sense to sign an agreement that provides how their property will be divided when and if the relationship ends. This assumes, of course, that the two of them have assets or will have assets.

The reasons for entering into an agreement are obviously not the same as those of a married couple. After all, the unmarried people have no automatic statutory share to be concerned about, no widow's or widower's allowance, no right to take against the will of the other, no preference for serving as

Marvin v. Marvin, 18 Cal. 3d 660, 557 P.2d 106, 134 Cal. Rptr. 815, in which the concept of "palimony" between unmarried persons was first brought to national attention.

†A woman involved in a prior "relationship" with Billie Jean King brought suit against her, seeking recovery for alleged broken promises.

executor or administrator. But if the living-together arrangement ends in a bitter dispute, an agreement for disposition of assets could be a financial and emotional lifesaver.

One of the big questions among PREMA signers—whether to insert a divorce contingency clause—does not of course exist for unmarried people. Thus they can say with no hesitation that their agreement is to be effective in all events, not just the death of one of the parties.

There is also the question of common-law marriages in some jurisdictions. A man and woman may want to affirmatively state in their agreement that they do *not* have a common-law marriage. The courts do not have to accept such an assertion, and of course a common-law marriage may arise after the written statement is made; but if the statement has been made in writing, there is at least some record of what the parties' intentions were at one time in their relationship.

Included in the State Laws section of Appendix 2 is the position of each state on the question of recognition of the right to enter into a common-law marriage.

For civil-law purposes a marriage is a marriage, and it may do no good to try to convince a partner to enter into a "premarital" agreement if in fact the parties are already husband and wife by a common-law marriage.

Though living-together arrangements are outside the main subject of this book, I have nonetheless included in Appendix 1 a general form that could be adapted for most purposes.

If you do execute such a document, remember that in cases where children have been born out of wedlock the court will have the power to order child support regardless of the terms of any agreement between the parents of the children. The court (in some states) could also declare that a common law marriage exists and could order payment of alimony, attorney fees, and distribution of property, all contrary to the provisions of the agreement signed between the parties. Though these things *could* all be done, the fact remains that the court, sitting in equity, will at least give *some* weight to the agreement and, absent other strong considerations, probably give *great* weight to the agreement signed by the couple.

Of course, there is nothing which says that two brothers or sisters, a parent and child, two widow friends, or others living together as a convenience could not enter into an agreement that will make things much easier for survivors upon the death of one of them or the breakup of their household. Likewise, any "other agreements" need not necessarily be limited to just two such individuals.

Recording such "other agreements" should not be a requirement unless real estate is involved, and then probably only the provisions relating to the real estate need be filed of record.

Good luck.

Appendix 1. Sample Forms

How to use the forms: Eight basic forms appear in Appendix 1. The first three are PREMAs, which we have discussed earlier in the book: Complete Mutual Release (page 88), Prior Property (page 91), and Combination (page 94). The fourth form is a Disclosure List (page 101), which may be used, probably with minor modifications, for any of the PREMAs. The fifth form is an Amendment, or Modification, form (page 103), which can be used with any of the three forms of PREMA. The sixth form (page 106) may be used to terminate any of the PREMAs. The seventh form (page 108) is a simple Property Division Agreement, which may be used by any persons sharing a household who are not planning marriage.

Before using the PREMA-related forms, turn to the State Laws section of Appendix 2 (page 113). In the State Laws section there is at least some citation of case law or statutory law and comment for each of the states. Since this law may change from time to time, you should follow the recommendations in Chapter 6 about local legal advice.

If after consulting your State Laws section you wish to take the calculated risk and insert a divorce contingency provision, thereby specifying that your PREMA is to be controlling in the event of divorce as well as death, a suggested provision is found in the eighth form (page 110). Such forms should be used in conjunction with a severability clause, which is included as a part of each suggested PREMA form.

Examples of various options are set out following several of the forms. These are by no means exclusive, and your PREMA will of course add and delete some language. In fitting the PREMA to your needs make sure to apply the guidelines which we discussed in the body of the book.

Have the notary check the acknowledgment on the form you use to make sure it is acceptable for your state (in Louisiana, "county" should be "parish," and in the District of Columbia there should be no reference to county).

Form 1. Complete Mutual Release PREMA

Premarital Agreement

THIS PREMARITAL AGREEMENT, made and entered into this ____ day of _____, 19____, by and between _____, of _____, _____, hereinafter called First Party, and _____, of _____, _____, hereinafter called Second Party, WITNESSETH:

Whereas the parties intend to marry, and in anticipation thereof desire to fix and determine by antenuptial, or premarital, agreement that each of them shall waive, relinquish, release, and renounce any and all claim in and to the property of the other after their marriage; and

Whereas there has been a full, fair, and adequate disclosure of assets of the parties, as well as full opportunity for independent legal counseling concerning the matters contained in this Agreement;

NOW, THEREFORE, it is agreed as follows:

1. Separate ownership of property. After the marriage of the parties each shall continue to hold and retain separate title and rights in and to any and all property each owns at the time of marriage or at any time acquired after their marriage. Each party acknowledges that the other shall have full and unrestricted right to sell, transfer, assign, encumber, or otherwise dispose of such separate property, and income therefrom (including interest, rents, dividends, and stock splits), free from any claim, demand, community property rights, or statutory interest of the other which might have arisen in any way because of the marriage of the parties.

Property "acquired after their marriage" as mentioned above refers to any and all items or assets which are replacements or exchanges for existing items or assets.

Any wages or earnings of the parties shall remain their separate property in all respects as described above.

2. Release of estate and election rights. The parties further waive,

relinquish, release, and renounce any and all rights each may have and later acquire as surviving spouse upon the death of the other, including any right of election to take against the will of the other, any right to claim an amount from the estate of the other if he or she should die intestate, any right to serve as executor or administrator of the other, and any and all other marital rights. It is the intention of the parties here that the property and estate of the other shall pass only to those specified in any last will and testament of the decedent, or to the decedent's lawful heirs in the event of intestacy, free and clear of claim, interest, widow's or widower's allowances, dower or curtesy rights, surviving spouse's homestead election rights, or other election rights they might otherwise have in respect to the will or estate of the other party.

Nothing herein shall be construed to constitute a release or waiver of any devise or bequest left to either by specific provision in the last will and testament of the other, nor a relinquishment of any property voluntarily transferred, or joint tenancy created, by the other. The parties affirmatively state, however, that no promises or representations have been made or received by either of them that any such bequest, devise, or transfers shall in fact be made to the other.

3. Disclosure of assets, informed and voluntary signing. The parties acknowledge that each has made good, fair, and adequate disclosure of his or her assets. The parties have discussed the nature and extent of the assets of each. First Party's present assets have a fair and reasonable market value of approximately $_____, and Second Party's present assets have a fair and reasonable market value of approximately $_____, all as summarized on the Disclosure List attached to this Agreement. Each party acknowledges that he or she has had adequate time to fully weigh the consequences of signing this Agreement, and has not been pressured, threatened, coerced, or unduly influenced to sign this Agreement. Each party has had full opportunity to obtain the benefit of independent legal counsel upon the matters in this Agreement, the applicable law, and the options available to him or her.

4. Signing necessary documents. The parties shall make, execute, and deliver any and all documents, including statutory waivers, consents, joinders, or releases necessary to effectuate their above-mentioned intentions.

5. Consideration. The consideration for this Agreement is the marriage of the parties and their mutual promises herein. In the event

the marriage does not take place, this Agreement shall have no force and effect whatsoever.

6. Binding nature of Agreement. This Agreement shall be binding upon and shall inure to the benefit of the parties, their heirs, executors, administrators, and personal representatives.

7. Entire Agreement, Amendment. This Agreement, including the attached Disclosure List, constitutes the entire understanding of the parties, and there are no other provisions, representations, or promises, express or implied, oral or written, other than as specifically set forth in this Agreement.

No amendment or termination relating to this Agreement shall be effective unless made in writing and executed by the parties with the same formalities as this Agreement.

8. Severability. In the event that any provision of this Agreement is held to be illegal, invalid, unenforceable, or against public policy, the remaining provisions of the Agreement shall nonetheless be considered valid and effective and shall be fully enforceable accordingly.

9. Controlling State law. This Agreement shall be construed and governed by the laws of the State of _____.

Dated and signed by the parties the year and day first set forth above.

First Party: Second Party:

_____   _____

State of _____
                              ss:
County of _____

On this ____ day of _____, 19___, before me, a notary public in and for said county and state, personally appeared _____ and _____ to me personally known, who did acknowledge that they signed the foregoing Agreement, and that they signed the same as their voluntary act and deed.

_____
Notary Public in and
for said County and State

My commission expires: _____

[ATTACH DISCLOSURE LIST]

Form 2. Prior Property PREMA

Premarital Agreement

THIS PREMARITAL AGREEMENT, made and entered into this _____ day of _____, 19____, by and between _____, of _____, _____, hereinafter called First Party, and _____, of _____, _____, hereinafter called Second Party, WITNESSETH:

Whereas the parties intend to marry, and in anticipation thereof desire to fix and determine by antenuptial, or premarital, agreement that each of them shall waive, relinquish, release, and renounce any and all claim or interest either may otherwise have acquired, by virtue of their marriage, in and to the property of the other owned or accumulated prior to the marriage; and

Whereas there has been a full, fair, and adequate disclosure of assets of the parties, as well as full opportunity for independent legal counseling concerning the matters contained in this Agreement;

NOW, THEREFORE, it is agreed as follows:

1. Separate ownership of property acquired prior to the marriage. After the marriage of the parties each shall continue to hold and retain separate title and rights in and to any and all property each owns at the time of marriage (hereinafter called Prior Property). Each party acknowledges that the other shall have full and unrestricted right to sell, transfer, assign, encumber, or otherwise dispose of such separate Prior Property, and income therefrom (including after-marriage interest, rents, dividends, and stock splits), free from any claim, demand, community property rights, or statutory interest of the other which might have arisen in any way because of the marriage of the parties.

Such separate ownership of Prior Property shall apply to any substitutions and replacements of such Prior Property during the marriage.

2. Release of estate and election rights to Prior Property The parties further waive, relinquish, release, and renounce any and all rights each may have and later acquire as surviving spouse upon the death of the other in and to such Prior Property, including any right of election to take against the will of the other, any right to claim any amount from the estate of the other if he or she should die intestate, and any right to serve as executor or administrator of the estate of the other, and any and all other marital rights regarding such marital

property. It is the intention of the parties here that the Prior Property of the other shall pass only to those specified in any last will and testament of the decedent, or to the decedent's lawful heirs in the event of intestacy, free and clear of claim, interest, widow's or widower's allowances, dower or curtesy rights, surviving spouse's homestead election rights, or election rights of the other regarding such Prior Property.

Nothing herein shall be construed to constitute a release or waiver of any devise or bequest left to either by specific provision in the last will and testament of the other, nor a relinquishment of any property voluntarily transferred, or joint tenancy created, by the other, nor a waiver of the right to serve as executor or personal representative of the estate of the other if subsequently specifically nominated under the last will and testament of the other. The parties affirmatively state, however, that no promises or representations have been made or received by either of them that any such bequest, devise, transfers, or nominations shall in fact be made in regard to the other.

3. Disclosure of assets, informed and voluntary signing. The parties acknowledge that each has made good, fair, and adequate disclosure of his or her assets which comprise such Prior Property. The parties have discussed the nature and extent of the assets of each. First Party's Prior Property assets have a fair and reasonable market value of approximately $_____, and Second Party's Prior Property assets have a fair and reasonable market value of approximately $_____, all as summarized on the Disclosure List attached to this Agreement. Each party acknowledges that he or she has had adequate time to fully weigh the consequences of signing this Agreement, and has not been pressured, threatened, coerced, or unduly influenced to sign this Agreement. Each party has had full opportunity to obtain the advice of independent counsel upon the matters in this Agreement, the applicable law, and the options available to him or her.

4. Signing necessary documents. The parties shall make, execute, and deliver any and all documents, including statutory waivers, consents, joinders, or releases necessary to effectuate their above-mentioned intentions.

5. Consideration. The consideration for this Agreement is the marriage of the parties and their mutual promises herein. In the event the marriage does not take place, this Agreement shall have no force and effect whatsoever.

6. After-acquired property not covered. None of the foregoing

provisions shall apply to property obtained by the parties after their marriage (except income, interest, rents, dividends, and stock splits from Prior Property). It is thus the specific declared intention of the parties that any and all property acquired by them after their marriage (except the aforesaid income from Prior Property) shall be treated in all respects as if this Agreement had never been executed. Any claims, demands, and interests which the parties own or acquire by virtue of their marriage shall exist in respect to such after-acquired property, including any dower, curtesy, widow's or widower's, survivor's, statutory, or election rights either has in the estate of the other upon death of such other party.

It is further understood that all wages and salaries and related earned income (as opposed to the previously mentioned passive income pertaining to Prior Property) of the parties shall be treated as if this Agreement had never been executed.

7. Binding nature of Agreement. This Agreement shall be binding upon and shall inure to the benefit of the parties, their heirs, executors, administrators, and personal representatives.

8. Entire Agreement, Amendment. This Agreement, including the attached Disclosure List, constitutes the entire understanding of the parties, and there are no other provisions, representations, or promises, express or implied, oral or written, other than as specifically set forth in this Agreement.

No modification, termination, or amendment relating to this Agreement shall be effective unless made in writing and executed by the parties with the same formalities as this Agreement.

9. Severability. In the event that any provision of this Agreement is held to be illegal, invalid, unenforceable, or against public policy, the remaining provisions of the Agreement shall nonetheless be considered valid and effective and shall be fully enforceable accordingly.

10. Controlling State law. This Agreement shall be construed and governed by the laws of the State of _____.

Dated and signed by the parties the year and day first set forth above.

First Party: Second Party:

_____   _____

State of _____
                 ss:
County of _____
On this ___ day of _____, 19___, before me, a notary public

in and for said county and state, personally appeared _____
and _____ to me personally known, who did acknowledge
that they signed the foregoing Agreement, and that they signed the
same as their voluntary act and deed.

_____
Notary Public in and
for said County and State

My commission expires: _____

[ATTACH DISCLOSURE LIST]

Note: The above form includes all passive income which is received after the marriage from Prior Property as within the definition of Prior Property. In other words, the spouses will not be sharing
with each other such income from prior-owned property. If you want
to change this so that such income will not be considered Prior
Property, it will be necessary to

1. delete this from the third full sentence of Paragraph 1: "and income therefrom (including after-marriage interest, rents, dividends, and stock splits),";
2. delete this from the first full sentence of Paragraph 6: "(except
   income, interest, rents, dividends, and stock splits from Prior
   Property)";
3. delete this from the second full sentence of Paragraph 6: "(except
   the aforesaid income from Prior Property)"; insert in place thereof: ", including any and all income from Prior Property,";
4. add this to the end of Paragraph 1: "Such ownership and use of
   Prior Property does not include income, interest, rents, dividends,
   and stock splits, which said income shall be considered after-
   acquired property, as treated in Paragraph 6 hereof."

Form 3. Combination PREMA

Premarital Agreement

THIS PREMARITAL AGREEMENT, made and entered into this
_____ day of _____, 19___, by and between _____, of
_____, _____, hereinafter called First Party, and

_____, of _____, _____, hereinafter
called Second Party, WITNESSETH:

Whereas the parties intend to marry, and in anticipation thereof
desire to fix and determine by antenuptial, or premarital, agreement
that each of them shall waive, relinquish, release, and renounce any
and all claim or interest either may otherwise have acquired, by
virtue of their marriage, in and to the property of the other accumulated prior to the marriage or after the marriage, and to receive
in place and in lieu thereof such property or payments as hereinafter
provided in this Agreement;

Whereas there has been a full, fair, and adequate disclosure of
assets of the parties, as well as full opportunity for independent legal
counseling concerning the matters contained in this Agreement;

NOW, THEREFORE, it is agreed as follows:

1. Separate ownership of property. After the marriage of the parties each shall continue to hold and retain separate title and rights
in and to any and all property each owns at the time of marriage or
at any time acquired after their marriage. Each party acknowledges
that the other shall have full and unrestricted right to sell, transfer,
assign, encumber, or otherwise dispose of such separate property
and income therefrom (including interest, rents, dividends, and
stock splits) free from any claim, demand, community property
rights, or statutory interest of the other which might have arisen in
any way because of the marriage of the parties, EXCEPT as provided
in Paragraph 3 hereof.

Such separate ownership of assets shall also apply to any substitutions and replacements of any prior-held assets during the marriage.

Further, any wages or earnings of the parties shall remain their
separate property in all respects as described above.

2. Release of marital, estate, and election rights. The parties further waive, relinquish, release, and renounce any and all rights each
may have and later acquire as surviving spouse upon the death of the
other, including any right of election to take against the will of the
other, and any right to claim an amount from the estate of the other
if he or she should die intestate, any right to act as executor or
administrator of the estate of the other, and any and all other marital
rights. It is the intention of the parties here that the property and
estate of the other shall pass only to those specified in any last will
and testament of the decedent, or to the decedent's lawful heirs in the
event of intestacy, free and clear of claim, interest, widow's or wid-

ower's allowances, dower or curtesy rights, surviving spouse's homestead election rights, or other election rights, EXCEPT as provided in Paragraph 3 hereof.

Nothing herein shall be construed to constitute a release or waiver of any devise or bequest left to either by specific provision in the last will and testament of the other, nor a relinquishment of any property voluntarily transferred, or joint tenancy created, nor a waiver of the right to serve as executor or personal representative of the estate of the other if subsequently specifically nominated under the last will and testament of the other. The parties affirmatively state, however, that no promises or representations have been made or received by either of them that any such bequest, devise, transfers, or nominations shall in fact be made to the other, except as specifically set forth in this Agreement.

3. Provision in lieu of marital rights. For and in consideration of the marriage of the parties, and their mutual promises herein, the following provision is made: [Here insert one or more types of options or combinations as listed in the Option Examples following this form.]

4. Disclosure of assets, informed and voluntary signing. The parties acknowledge that each has made good, fair, and adequate disclosure of his or her assets. The parties have discussed the nature and extent of the assets of each. First Party's present assets have a fair and reasonable market value of approximately $_____$, and Second Party's present assets have a fair and reasonable market value of approximately $_____$, all as summarized on the Disclosure List attached to this Agreement. Each party acknowledges that he or she has had adequate time to fully weigh the consequences of signing this Agreement, and has not been pressured, threatened, coerced, or unduly influenced to sign this Agreement. Each party has had full opportunity to obtain the benefit of independent legal counsel upon the matters in this Agreement, the applicable law, and the options available to him or her.

5. Consideration. The consideration for this Agreement is the marriage of the parties and their mutual promises herein. In the event the marriage does not take place this Agreement shall have no force and effect whatsoever.

6. Signing necessary documents. The parties shall make, execute, and deliver any and all documents, including statutory waivers, necessary to effectuate their above-mentioned intentions. Further, the appropriate executor, administrator, agent, trustee, or personal rep-

resentative of the parties is authorized and directed to perform all acts necessary to accomplish the goals set forth in Paragraph 3 hereof.

7. Binding nature of Agreement. This Agreement shall be binding upon and shall inure to the benefit of the parties, their heirs, executors, administrators, and personal representatives.

8. Entire Agreement, Amendment. This Agreement, including the attached Disclosure List, constitutes the entire understanding of the parties, and there are no other provisions, representations, or promises, express or implied, oral or written, other than as specifically set forth in this Agreement.

No modification, termination, or amendment relating to this Agreement shall be effective unless made in writing and executed by the parties with the same formalities as this Agreement.

9. Severability. In the event that any provision of this Agreement is held to be illegal, invalid, unenforceable, or against public policy, the remaining provisions of the Agreement shall nonetheless be considered valid and effective and shall be fully enforceable accordingly.

10. Controlling State law. This Agreement shall be construed and governed by the laws of the State of _____.

Dated and signed by the parties the year and day first set forth above.

First Party: Second Party:

_____   _____

State of _____
                        ss:
County of _____
On this ____ day of _____, 19____, before me, a notary public in and for said county and state, personally appeared _____ and _____ to me personally known, who did acknowledge that they signed the foregoing Agreement, and that they signed the same as their voluntary act and deed.

                              _____
                              Notary Public in and
                              for said County and State

My commission expires: _____

[ATTACH DISCLOSURE LIST]

Option Examples. One or more of these types of options may be inserted for the benefit of the spouse who gives up the most by relinquishing his or her marital rights. If more than one such provision is used, each should be designated as a separate subparagraph (i.e., a), b), c), etc.).

- Provision of insurance for spouse:

"First Party shall obtain, within thirty days of the marriage of the parties, life insurance upon First Party's life in an amount not less than $150,000, with Second Party named as beneficiary thereon. First Party shall not change said beneficiary, shall pay all premiums due upon said policy during the life of First Party, and shall further provide through First Party's will that all proceeds of said insurance policy shall pass free and clear of any and all estate and inheritance taxes."

Note: The type of life insurance can be specified, such as whole life, universal life, or term.

- Transfer of sum to spouse:

"First Party shall, within thirty days of the date of marriage of the parties, transfer to Second Party the sum of $50,000."

Note: Annual or other installment payments may be specified.

- Transfer of nonmonetary property to spouse:

"First Party shall, within forty-five days of the date of marriage of the parties, transfer to Second Party the unencumbered title to one new automobile of Second Party's choice, with a purchase price of not less than $15,000."

Note: Any number of days may be specified, and of course *any* property, account, or monies may be described.

- One party will move into the home owned by the other after their marriage. The owner agrees to transfer one-half ownership to the other so that he/she will not feel like a renter in the house as the years go by. In return, the new half-owner will give a note and mortgage to the other so that the transferor's children will receive something for the one-half interest someday:

"Second Party shall, within twenty days of the date of marriage of the parties, transfer to First Party title to one half of Second Party's interest in and to Second Party's home located at 605 Belmont Blvd., Pittsburgh, Pennsylvania. Contemporaneously therewith, First Party shall make, execute, and deliver to Second Party a promissory note in the amount of $60,000, secured by a real estate mortgage upon First Party's one-half interest in said property, payable at the death of Second Party, without interest upon said promissory note."

Note: This provision allows a spouse to have an interest in a home immediately without having to pay for it except on the death of the other, at which time its value will probably have appreciated. The interest-free promissory note may well constitute a gift, but will qualify for the marital deduction.

Note: If the deed creates a joint tenancy with right of survivorship or a tenancy by the entirety, the surviving spouse will come into full ownership of the property by operation of law upon the death of the first to die. This would not occur if, for example, a tenancy in common were created. Even if a joint-tenancy interest were not created by the original deed, a later deed could accomplish the same thing. Also, a later transfer by will or a grant of option to buy in a will might be considered.

• Agreement that spouse shall receive a portion of the estate of the other, except a smaller percentage than given by statute:

"That if First Party should die during the marriage of the parties at a time prior to Second Party's death, Second Party shall receive 15 percent of First Party's net estate, free and clear of any and all estate and inheritance taxes. 'Net estate' for this calculation shall refer to the gross estate of First Party, less expenses for estate administration, funeral, burial, valid claims against the estate, outstanding mortgages, notes or liens upon gross assets of the estate, and income or real estate taxes accrued but not paid prior to the death of First Party."

Note: Here the parties have arrived at a percentage which they feel is fair under the circumstances. Considering everything, 15 percent may be much fairer than the one third or one half or more which the law would otherwise require pass to the survivor.

• Agreement to accept will devise or bequest in lieu of other marital rights in estate of deceased spouse:

"That Second Party agrees to accept any and all bequest or devise made in First Party's will for the benefit of Second Party in lieu of any and all statutory, dower, or curtesy rights, surviving spouse's homestead election or other election rights, widow or widower's allowances, or any and all other marital rights owned or later accrued on behalf of Second Party, including the right to serve as executor or personal representative of the estate of First Party. First Party must die testate for this Agreement to be effective."

Note: Here the Second Party relies entirely on the fairness of First Party without knowing what might be later given to him or her by will. If First Party fails to leave anything to the other, it may, but would not necessarily, constitute grounds for attacking the PREMA. Remember that even with the best of intentions problems could arise if First Party dies or becomes incompetent before the will is executed.

Note: If this option is used, it would be very dangerous for First Party to leave Second Party a paltry sum or a sum which would appear to be unreasonably small considering the standard of living and relative assets of the parties.

- Provision of trust for benefit of spouse:

"That First Party shall create a trust, either by last will and testament or by inter vivos act, which will consist of a corpus of not less than $100,000, for the benefit of Second Party. Under the terms of said trust Second Party shall receive all of the income thereof, payable in quarterly installments during the life of Second Party. Second Party shall have full power of appointment regarding said trust. In the event Second Party fails to exercise her power of appointment regarding said trust, or the remainder thereof, any balance thereof shall pass according to the residuary provisions of First Party's last will and testament. First Party shall provide in his last will and testament that said trust amount shall be free and clear of any estate and inheritance taxes in regard to First Party's estate."

Note: A great variety of trusts may be set up for the surviving spouse.

- Agreement to take marital share from specific property:

"That Second Party agrees that she shall receive an amount equal to her full statutory share as a surviving spouse of Second Party under applicable state law at the time of First Party's death. In no event, however, shall such value be taken in the form of corporate stock of XYZ Family Corporation [or Blackacre Family Farm; or the personal residence located at 1292 Kelly Lane, Kansas City, Kansas]."

Note: Here the spouse receives the full statutory share; he or she simply agrees not to take it out of certain assets, such as a going family business.

Form 4. Disclosure List (to be attached to all PREMAs)

Disclosure List

The following is a general list of assets, using estimated values. No attempt is made here to set forth every individual item owned by the parties. The intention is to give each party a fair, full, and adequate disclosure of assets by category.

First Party

Category	Gross Value	Encumbrance	Net Value
1. Real Estate			
a) Personal Residence	$	$	$
b) Other, Improved	$	$	$
c) Other, Unimproved	$	$	$
2. Personal Property			
a) Accounts, Cash	$	$	$
b) Stocks, Bonds	$	$	$
c) Vehicles	$	$	$
d) Jewelry, Household Goods, Collections, Misc.	$	$	$
e) Life insurance (Paid-up value)	$	$	$
TOTALS	$	$	$

---

3. Additional factors or considerations disclosed (retirement plans, IRAs, trusts, probable substantial inheritances, etc. Also, debts not listed):

Second Party

Category	Gross Value	Encumbrance	Net Value
1. Real Estate			
a) Personal Residence	$	$	$
b) Other, Improved	$	$	$
c) Other, Unimproved	$	$	$
2. Personal Property			
a) Accounts, Cash	$	$	$
b) Stocks, Bonds	$	$	$
c) Vehicles	$	$	$
d) Jewelry, Household Goods, Collections, Misc.	$	$	$
e) Life Insurance (Paid-up value)	$	$	$
TOTALS	$	$	$

3. Additional factors or considerations disclosed (retirement plans, IRAs, trusts, probable substantial inheritances, etc. Also, debts not listed):

_____

Read, signed, and made a part of the Premarital Agreement to which it is attached this ____ day of _____, 19____.

First Party: Second Party:

_____   _____

Note: This form must be attached to the premarital agreement to which it applies.

Note: The above form *summarizes* the categories and subcategories. If you wish to *itemize* each asset, you may of course do so, using the Form 4 disclosure list as a guideline for your categories.

Note: If the parties are entering into a Property Division Agreement instead of a PREMA, this document may be used as a general guideline, but it should be called an Asset Description List and need not include intangible assets such as accounts, stocks, bonds, and life insurance. It would also not be necessary to list debts, unless they are joint debts with the other member of the household. On the other hand, household *things,* such as collections, appliances, furniture, antiques, and even jewelry, should be listed in detail, with periodic updates (which should be dated and initialed or signed). Of course, if the finances of the parties are more intertwined, then the Asset Description List should elaborate accordingly.

Form 5. Amendment (Modification) to PREMA

Amendment to Premarital Agreement

THIS AMENDMENT TO PREMARITAL AGREEMENT, made and entered into this ____ day of _____, 19____, by and between _____, hereinafter called First Party, and _____, hereinafter called Second Party, both of _____, _____, WITNESSETH:

Whereas the parties have heretofore entered into a Premarital Agreement dated _____, 19____, and now wish to amend said Premarital Agreement and to reduce said amendment to writing;

NOW, THEREFORE, it is agreed as follows:

1. That for good, valuable, and sufficient consideration (including the mutually expressed agreement of the parties herein and the love and affection of the parties for each other), receipt of all of which is hereby acknowledged, the parties hereby amend the aforesaid Premarital Agreement dated _____, 19____, as follows: [Here insert amendment(s). See Amendment Examples following this Form.]

2. That in all other respects not expressly amended herein said Premarital Agreement is ratified and confirmed.

3. That there has been full, fair, and adequate disclosure in all respects as if this had been an original Premarital Agreement. Further, the parties have had full opportunity to obtain independent legal counsel to the full extent required by law.

Dated and signed by the parties the year and day first set forth above.

First Party: Second Party:

_____   _____

State of _____
                        ss:
County of _____
On this ____ day of _____, 19____, before me, a notary public
in and for said county and state, personally appeared _____
and _____, to me personally known, who did acknowledge
that they signed the foregoing Amendment To Premarital Agreement, and that they signed the same as their voluntary act and deed.

                         _____
                         Notary Public in and
                         for said County and State

My commission expires: _____

Amendment Examples. Amendments to a PREMA will often take
the form of *deleting* an old provision and *inserting* a new one.

• To delete an old provision (say, Paragraph 6) add the following
subparagraph to Paragraph 1 above:
  "By deleting Paragraph 6 thereof."

• To delete part of an old provision:
  "By deleting the last sentence of Paragraph 4 thereof."

• To substitute a new provision for an old one:
  "By deleting, in Paragraph 2 thereof, the phrase 'and any right to
act as executor or administrator of the estate of the other.', and
inserting in place thereof the following: 'except the right to serve as
executor or administrator of the estate of the other.'."

• To add a new provision without deleting an old one. Assume Sub-
paragraphs a) through c) already exist in Paragraph 3 of a Combination PREMA:
  "By inserting the following at the end of Paragraph 3 thereof:
    d) That any and all amounts which Second Party shall re-
       ceive from First Party under the provisions of this
       Premarital Agreement shall be net, free and clear of any
       and all estate or inheritance taxes thereon."

- To add a provision giving household goods to a surviving spouse in, say, a Combination PREMA:

"By inserting the following at the end of Paragraph 3 thereof:
  d) That Second Party shall receive as her own property any and all household goods within the home at 230 Lancaster Boulevard, Chicago, Illinois, at the time of First Party's death."

- To add a provision giving Second Party the option to buy First Party's home after First Party's death:

"By inserting the following as Paragraph 4 thereof, at the same time designating existing Paragraphs 4, 5, and 6 to be Paragraphs 5, 6, and 7 respectively:
  4. That Second Party shall have, after First Party's death, the option to purchase First Party's home located at 455 Belmont St., New York, New York, legally described as Lot 22, Block 5, Hilton Subdivision, New York, New York, for the sum of Twenty-five Thousand Dollars ($25,000). If said option to purchase is exercised, Second Party shall deliver written notice to First Party's personal representative of said intention to exercise said option, all within thirty days of the death of First Party. Thereafter, First Party's personal representative shall make, execute, and deliver to Second Party all First Party's right, title, and interest in and to the above-described real estate upon receipt of payment from Second Party of the aforesaid sum of $25,000. In adding this provision First Party acknowledges that said option price is very substantially less than the present fair and reasonable market value of said real estate."

Note: The last sentence above should only be inserted where the option price is in fact below the market price.

- To add to the Disclosure List attached to a PREMA an asset which was overlooked at the time of the signing of the original Agreement:

"By deleting, in Paragraph 1.c) of First Party's Disclosure List, the sum of $5,000 as the Gross Value and Net Value of the Other, Unimproved real estate there shown, and inserting in place thereof the sum of $50,000. The parties acknowledge that First Party's insertion of the incorrect figure in the original Premarital Agreement was unintentional, and Second Party further acknowledges that she

105

would have executed said Premarital Agreement even if the correct figure had been inserted in the original Disclosure List."

Note: In Paragraph 3 of the Amendment form there is a recitation to the effect that there has been full opportunity to obtain independent legal counsel to the full extent required by law. In point of fact, if the amendment gives additional property to the less wealthy spouse, or otherwise increases the share to such spouse, the requirement of independent legal counsel becomes less important (unless of course the change is so generous that there is a danger that someone could contend that undue influence, etc., has been practiced against an old, enfeebled, ill, or incompetent wealthy spouse). And obviously if there is an attempt to more severely restrict the transfer of property to the poorer spouse, questions about adequacy of consideration and independent legal counsel could well arise.

Form 6. Termination Agreement

Termination Agreement

THIS TERMINATION AGREEMENT, made and entered into this ____ day of _____, 19____, by and between _____ and _____, both residents of _____, _____,
WITNESSETH:

Whereas the parties have heretofore entered into a Premarital Agreement dated _____, 19____, and now wish to terminate said Premarital Agreement and to reduce said termination to writing;

NOW, THEREFORE, it is agreed as follows:

1. That for good, valuable, and sufficient consideration (including the mutual promises of the parties herein and the love and affection of the parties for each other), receipt of all of which is hereby acknowledged, the parties hereby terminate, cancel, and set aside in its entirety the aforesaid Premarital Agreement entered into between them on _____, 19____, a copy of which is attached hereto for reference.

2. That any prior transfers of property or property rights of the parties made in reliance upon said Premarital Agreement shall not be affected by this termination unless the parties hereafter separately and independently act to retransfer or otherwise negate any such prior transfers.

3. That each party acknowledges that he or she has had adequate time to fully weigh the consequences of signing this Termination Agreement, has had full opportunity to obtain independent legal counsel, and has not been pressured, threatened, coerced, or unduly influenced to sign this Termination Agreement. No promises have been made in connection with this Termination Agreement except: [Here state any promises. If none, state "None".]

4. That this document sets forth the entire Termination Agreement between the parties and cannot be orally changed or modified in any way.

Dated and signed by the parties the year and day first set forth above.

Husband: Wife:

_____   _____

State of _____
                              ss:
County of _____

On this ____ day of _____, 19____, before me, a notary public in and for said county and state, personally appeared _____ and _____ to me personally known, who did acknowledge that they signed the foregoing Termination Agreement, and that they signed the same as their voluntary act and deed.

_____
Notary Public in and
for said County and State

My commission expires:_____

Note: An example of the type of promise which might be made in the event of termination, as alluded to in Paragraph 3, would be the agreement to make immediate payment of money or transfer of property by one to the other in return for terminating the PREMA.

Note: If the wealthy spouse is in poor health or has questionable mental capacity, the use of independent legal counsel—or at least use of the wealthy person's legal counsel—is often a good idea when a Termination Agreement is signed.

Form 7. Property Division Agreement for Persons Not Intending Marriage

Property Division Agreement

THIS AGREEMENT, made and entered into this ____ day of
_____, 19____, by and between _____, hereinafter
called First Party, and _____, hereinafter called Second
Party, WITNESSETH:

Whereas the parties intend to share living accommodations, and
are unmarried, and wish to reduce to writing their respective rights
and obligations and to provide for the division of property and things
in the event of termination of said living accommodation arrangement between themselves;

NOW, THEREFORE, it is agreed as follows:

1. Separate ownership of property. The parties shall at all times
continue to hold and retain separate title and rights in and to any and
all property each owns prior to or after they enter into said living
accommodation arrangement. Each party acknowledges that the
other shall have full and unrestricted right to sell, transfer, assign, or
otherwise dispose of such separate property, and income therefrom,
free and clear of any claim or demand of the other.

It is further agreed that such separate ownership of assets shall
apply to any substitutions and replacements of assets held at the time
the parties began such living accommodation arrangement.

2. Marital status. The parties acknowledge that they are not husband and wife and that this document is not to be considered to be
an antenuptial, or premarital, agreement. No promises are made
herein which are contingent upon, or which anticipate, any marriage
between the parties.

3. Listing of assets. Attached to this Agreement are the respective
asset description lists of the parties disclosing the assets which each
will be using and/or sharing in said living accommodation arrangement. Possession of these assets and any other assets contributed
during the living accommodation arrangement shall be returned to
each person upon any termination of said living accommodation
arrangement.

4. Disclosure of assets. The parties acknowledge that the value of
their assets is immaterial to, and affects in no way, the validity of this
Agreement. They have discussed (have not discussed) [Delete one]

the general extent of the assets of each other. They acknowledge that since neither party seeks nor shall seek any assets of the other upon any termination of their living accommodation arrangement, the nature and extent of their other assets need not be disclosed.

5. Other provisions. [Here insert any applicable options as listed below or as otherwise considered appropriate.]

6. Binding nature of Agreement. This Agreement shall be binding upon and shall inure to the benefit of the parties, their heirs, executors, administrators, and personal representatives.

7. Entire Agreement. This Agreement, including any attached asset description list, constitutes the entire understanding of the parties, and there are no other provisions, representations, or promises, express or implied, oral or written, other than as specifically set forth herein. This Agreement may be amended only by a written document signed by both parties before a notary public duly authorized within the state of signature.

8. Severability. In the event that any provision of this Agreement is held to be illegal, invalid, unenforceable, or against public policy, the remaining provisions of the Agreement shall nonetheless be considered valid and effective and shall be fully enforceable accordingly.

Dated and signed by the parties the year and day first set forth above.

First Party: Second Party:

_____   _____

State of _____
              ss:
County of _____

On this ___ day of _____, 19___, before me, a notary public in and for said county and state, personally appeared _____ and _____ to me personally known, who did acknowledge that they signed the foregoing Agreement, and that they signed the same as their voluntary act and deed.

                        _____

                        Notary Public in and
                        for said County and State

My commission expires: _____

[ATTACH ASSET DISCLOSURE LIST]

Note: The reference to marital status and intentions may be omitted where inappropriate (brothers, sisters, etc., or persons of same sex).

Note: In Paragraph 5 may be inserted the parties' plans for sale of jointly owned property, options to purchase such jointly owned property, provisions (if any) for return of certain gifts to each other, statements regarding nonliability of debts of each other and statements regarding joint liability for payment of utilities upon breakup of the household, and any related matters.

Note: This form is *not* a contract defining the rights and obligations of the parties while living together—though such provisions could be added. It sets forth the status of the parties and procedures for disposition of the property upon termination of the arrangement.

Form 8. Divorce Contingency Provision

[Insert paragraph number.] The parties hereto contemplate a happy and lasting marriage which will be terminated only by the death of one of the parties. In the unfortunate event that the marriage should be terminated by divorce (dissolution) for any reason, regardless of fault, jurisdiction, or which party is petitioner, the following shall apply: [Here insert appropriate language. See options below for examples.]

Both parties acknowledge that they have discussed this provision; that it is fair; and that its inclusion is an inducement to marriage of the parties under the circumstances.

Option Examples.
• If the PREMA is a Complete Mutual Release PREMA, one could simply state: "That the waivers, relinquishments, releases, and renunciations of the parties in and to the property, income, and wages of the other as herein set forth shall apply with full force and effect to any possible claim for property, alimony, or attorney fees of or from the other."

• If the PREMA is a Prior Property PREMA: "That the waivers, relinquishments, releases, and renunciations of the parties in and to the Prior Property of the other as herein set forth shall apply with full force and effect to any possible claim for property, alimony, or attorney fees of or from the other in respect to such Prior Property.

Further, that any property acquired through the joint efforts of the parties after the marriage shall be divided equally."

- If the PREMA is a Combination PREMA: "That the waivers, relinquishments, releases, and renunciations of the parties in and to the property, income, and wages of the other as herein set forth shall apply with full force and effect to any possible claim for property, alimony, or attorney fees of or from the other, EXCEPT that Second Party shall receive _____."

Note: Try to ensure that the provision for the spouse is not "unconscionable." One must also be careful that the provision not be for proportionately *more* than the spouse would have received if she, say, had stayed in the marriage, because it then might be attacked as being "an incitement to divorce."

Note: Since there is a recitation that the parties have discussed this general divorce contingency provision, make sure that such a discussion in fact takes place.

Appendix 2. State Laws

Alabama

1. *General comment:* Alabama has adopted the waiver provisions of the Uniform Probate Code, which allow a surviving spouse to waive marital rights in writing after fair disclosure.

Prior Alabama statutes and case law also allowed premarital agreements where adequate consideration existed and full disclosure was made.

2. *Divorce contingency provision allowed?* Unknown.
3. *Common-law marriage state?* Yes.
4. *Community property state?* No.
5. *Legal authorities and references:* Code of Alabama, Section 43-8-72; Allison v. Stevens, 269 Ala. 288, 112 So.2d 457 (1959); Hamilton v. Hamilton, 255 Ala. 284, 51 So.2d 13 (1950); Norrell v. Thompson, 252 Ala. 603, 42 So.2d 461 (1949); Rash v. Bogart, 226 Ala. 284, 146 So. 814 (1933); Merchants' National Bank of Mobile v. Hubbard, 222 Ala. 518, 133 So. 723 (1931); Crownover v. Crownover, 216 Ala. 286, 113 So. 42 (1927); Richter v. Richter, 180 Ala. 218, 60 So. 880 (1913).

Alaska

1. *General comment:* Alaska has adopted the waiver provisions of the Uniform Probate Code, which allow a surviving spouse to waive marital rights in writing after fair disclosure.

Alaska has very little case law in this area.

2. *Divorce contingency provision allowed?* Unknown.
3. *Common-law marriage state?* No.

4. *Community property state?* No.

5. *Legal authorities and references:* Alaska Statutes, Section 13.-11.085.

Arizona

1. *General comment:* In 1974 Arizona adopted the general waiver provisions of the Uniform Probate Code, which allow a surviving spouse to waive marital rights in writing after fair disclosure.

2. *Divorce contingency provision allowed?* Uncertain in a particular case; however, there is case law to the effect that agreements which provide for or tend to induce divorce are contrary to public policy and unenforceable.

3. *Common-law marriage state?* No.

4. *Community property state?* Yes. In addition to the usual waiver language in the statute there is a provision which reads: "A waiver of all rights does not affect the rights of each spouse to his share of community property, in the absence of a contrary provision; but a complete settlement terminates rights to community property in assets then owned or thereafter acquired, unless the settlement agreement provides to the contrary."

Thus, anyone who wishes to waive all rights, including community property rights, must be very specific about it under Arizona law. The waiver provisions in the forms in this book are in fact very specific on this point.

5. *Legal authorities and references:* Arizona Revised Statutes, Section 14-2204; Matter of Beaman's Estate (App. 1978) 119 Ariz. 614, 583 P.2d 270; Spector v. Spector, 23 Ariz.App. 131, 531 P.2d 176 (1975); Ellis v. C.I.R., 437 F.2d 442 (1971); Smith v. Tang, 100 Ariz. 196, 412 P.2d 697 (1966).

Arkansas

1. *General comment:* Arkansas allows PREMAs when there has been full disclosure, good faith, and when the agreement is not considered promotive of divorce. The Arkansas experience is based on case law rather than statutes. Several PREMAs have been stricken down because of overreaching by the prospective husband, because the wife was inexperienced in financial matters, because there was no independent legal counsel, or because a divorce contingency clause in the PREMA was held to be against public policy.

2. *Divorce contingency provision allowed?* Yes, if done properly. If the language of the PREMA indicates that the document will apply only in the event of divorce, or that a divorce was contemplated, the PREMA may be stricken down as "promotive of divorce." But the Arkansas Supreme Court has in recent years shown a tendency to accept divorce contingency provisions if they are simply part of a clause which covers *all* contingencies (i.e., death *or* divorce).

It is believed that the divorce contingency provision suggested in the forms in this book would be considered proper if used with the rest of the basic format of the forms.

3. *Common-law marriage state?* No.

4. *Community property state?* No.

5. *Legal authorities and references:* Dingledine v. Dingledine, 258 Ark. 204, 523 S.W.2d 189 (1975); Hughes v. Hughes, 251 Ark. 63, 471 S.W.2d 355 (1971); LeFevers v. LeFevers, 240 Ark. 992, 403 S.W.2d 65 (1966); Bonner v. Bonner, 204 Ark. 1006, 166 S.W.2d 254 (1942); Burnes v. Burnes, Adm'r., 203 Ark. 334, 157 S.W.2d 24 (1941); Davis v. Davis, 196 Ark. 57, 116 S.W.2d 607 (1938); Oliphant v. Oliphant, 177 Ark. 613, 7 S.W.2d 783 (1928); 24 Arkansas Law Review 275.

California

1. *General comment:* The state of California has been the most active in the nation in enacting legislation dealing with premarital agreements. In January 1985 California enacted a very comprehensive law relating to PREMAs. The law was clumsily written and was sure to have raised questions which would have to be answered by amendment or judicial construction.

Written "waivers" and "agreements" were to be enforceable unless the surviving spouse proved that a fair and reasonable disclosure of property and obligations was not made *unless* the surviving spouse waived such fair and reasonable disclosure *after* advice by independent legal counsel, *or* unless such surviving spouse was not represented at all when the document was signed.

Impressed upon the above law was a provision that allowed a court to enforce waivers and agreements if the overall result is fair and reasonable and enforcement would not be "unconscionable." The court was given great latitude in selecting between those provisions or parts of provisions which are deemed conscionable or unconscionable.

Under the 1985 and 1986 California law, then, it was a practical necessity for each party to retain independent legal counsel for all original waivers or agreements and changes thereto.

But in L.1985, Chapter 1315, California enacted the substance of the Uniform Premarital Agreement Act. This will considerably simplify and clarify the California situation, as explained in the comments regarding the Uniform Act in chapter 2. See page 145 for the text of the Uniform Act.

2. *Divorce contingency provision allowed?* Yes, unless the court finds that the agreement is an inducement to divorce. In a recent case the California Court of Appeals, 6th District, declared that a PREMA was invalid as against public policy because it awarded the woman a half-million dollars and a house only in the event she obtained a divorce. In other words, instead of defining the rights of the parties, it granted the woman what was, in effect, a reward for divorcing her husband.

The just-passed Uniform Premarital Agreement Act allows divorce contingency provisions. Best practice, though, would be to be careful in not appearing to "reward" a party with property or payments which will take effect *only* in the event of divorce.

3. *Common-law marriage state?* No.

4. *Community property state?* Yes.

5. *Legal authorities and references:* California Laws, 1985, Chapter 1315; California Probate Code, Part 3, Chapter 1 (Sections 140–47), Chapter 2, and Chapter 3; In Re Noghrey, 11 Fam.L.Rep. (BNA) 1459 (Cal.Ct.App. 1985); In Re Marriage of Dawley, 17 Cal.3d 342, 551 P.2d 323, 131 Cal.Rptr 3 (1976); In Re Higgason's Marriage, 110 Cal.Rptr 897, 516 P.2d 289 (1973); Re Brisacher's Estate, 172 Cal.App.2d 95, 183 P.2d 329 (1959), remittitur ordered on other grounds, 175 Cal.App. 2d 370, 346 P.2d 225; Barker v. Barker, 293 P.2d 85 (Cal. 1956); In Re Wamack's Estate, 137 Cal.App.2d 112, 289 P.2d 871 (1955); Re Howe's Estate, 81 Cal.App.2d 95, 183 P.2d 329 (1947); Re Schwartz's Estate, 79 Cal.App.2d 308, 179 P.2d 868 (1947); Re Shapero's Estate, 39 Cal. App.2d 144, 102 P.2d 569 (1940); Re Warner's Estate, 158 Cal. 441, 111 P. 352 (1910); 11 USFL Rev. 317 (1977).

Colorado

1. *General comment:* Colorado has enacted the general waiver provisions of the Uniform Probate Code, which allow a surviving spouse to waive marital rights in writing after fair disclosure.

2. *Divorce contingency provision allowed?* Yes, although the

Colorado Court of Appeals has held that a PREMA which attempts to limit or eliminate future alimony in the event of divorce is void as being contrary to public policy. The Colorado courts have drawn a distinction between the right to fix and determine property rights existing *before* a marriage (which is allowed by PREMA) and property and spousal maintenance rights which may have matured *during* a marriage (which is not allowed by PREMA). Colorado is perhaps the only state which stresses this particular perceived difference.

3. *Common-law marriage state?* Yes.

4. *Community property state?* No.

5. *Legal authorities and references:* Colorado Revised Statutes, Section 15-11-204; Re Estate of Lebsock, 618 P.2d 683 (Colo.App. 1980); In Re Marriage of Newman, 44 Colo.App. 307, 616 P.2d 982 (1980); In Re Marriage of Stokes, 43 Colo.App. 451, 608 P.2d 824 (1979); In Re Marriage of Ingels, 42 Colo.App. 245, 596 P.2d 1211 (1979); Maher v. Knauss, 150 Colo. 108, 370 P.2d 1017 (1962); In Re Griffee's Estate, 108 Colo. 366, 117 P.2d 823 (1941); Re Bradley's Estate, 106 Colo. 500, 106 P.2d 1063 (1940).

Connecticut

1. *General comment:* Connecticut allows PREMAs under the general rules pertaining to fairness and disclosure recognized throughout the jurisdictions. Connecticut recognizes the right to waive marital shares in the very same section of the statute which provides for the marital share itself. It states that the spousal share "shall not apply to any case in which, by written contract made before or after the marriage, either party has received from the other what was intended as a provision in lieu of such statutory share."

2. *Divorce contingency provision allowed?* Yes, although case law indicates that the court might strike down any PREMA provision which attempts to relieve a spouse's duty of spousal support *during* the marriage or the duty to support minor children *after* a divorce.

3. *Common-law marriage state?* No.

4. *Community property state?* No.

5. *Legal authorities and references:* Connecticut General Statutes, Section 46-12; McHugh v. McHugh, 181 Conn. 482, 436 A.2d 8 (1980); Parniaski v. Parniaski, 33 Conn.Supp. 44, 359 A.2d 719 (1976); Appeal of Cowles, 74 Conn. 24, 49 A. 195 (1901); Re Baker's Appeal, 56 Conn. 586 (1888).

Delaware

1. *General comment:* Delaware allows PREMAs under the general rules relating to fairness and disclosure applied throughout the jurisdictions. Although a Delaware statute requires that such "marriage contract" be executed in writing before two witnesses at least ten days before marriage, the Delaware court has held that PREMAs are not solely creatures of statute and that no particular form is necessary for validity.

Delaware law also requires that any PREMA or POSTMA concerning real estate be recorded in the county where the property is situated within one year of the making of the contract. Failure to so record means that the PREMA shall not be effective as against third parties without notice.

2. *Divorce contingency provision allowed?* Uncertain. On the one hand the statute only authorizes PREMAs to determine rights in the parties' estates "during marriage and after its dissolution *by death.*" On the other hand, the Delaware courts have made point of the fact, as mentioned above, that PREMAs are not solely creatures of statute.

3. *Common-law marriage state?* No.

4. *Community property state?* No.

5. *Legal authorities and references:* 13 Delaware Code, Section 301; Tyre v. Lewis, 276 A.2d 747 (Del. 1971); Hill v. Hill, 262 A.2d 661, aff'd Del.Supr., 269 A.2d 212 (1970); Cochran v. McBeath, 1 Del.Ch. 187 (1822).

Florida

1. *General comment:* Florida allows an individual to waive marital rights, by written agreement or waiver, before or after the marriage. Florida's statute is unusual in at least two respects: First, "fair disclosure" is required only "if the agreement, contract, or waiver is executed *after* the marriage," with "no disclosure . . . required . . . before marriage"; and second, no consideration other than the execution of the document itself is said to be necessary to its validity, whether executed before *or after* the marriage.

In spite of Florida's statute, case law and good practice suggest fair disclosure is the safer course to follow. For example, a recent case states that this statute does not protect one who "voluntarily averts the truth and thereby misleads a party into contracting marriage." Also, Florida case law has held that the nondisclosure rule regarding PREMAs is found in the *Probate Code,* and is therefore not applicable to PREMAs involved in *dissolution of marriage* actions. Thus it is recommended that anyone who wants to take advantage of a divorce contingency provision must still follow the general rules regarding disclosure.

2. *Divorce contingency provision allowed?* Yes. Florida is recognized as probably the most progressive state in the country in the allowance of divorce contingency provisions in PREMAs. The Florida cases, and especially the *Posner* case, cited below, are widely quoted throughout the jurisdictions. In *Posner* the Florida court noted that some of the old reasons mainly advanced for opposing divorce contingency provisions (such as the supposed encitement or encouragement of divorce) are pretty much meaningless in this day of high divorce rates and no-fault divorce.

3. *Common-law marriage state?* No.

4. *Community property state?* No.

5. *Legal authorities and references:* Florida Probate Code, Section 732.702; Moldofsky v. Stregack, 449 So.2d 918 (App.4 Dist. Fla. 1984); Topper v. Stewart, 449 So.2d 373 (App.3 Dist. Fla. 1984); Ellis First Nat. Bank of West Pasco v. Downing, 443 So.2d 337 (App.2 Dist. Fla. 1983); Coleman v. Estate of Coleman, 439 So.2d 1016 (App.1 Dist. Fla. 1983); In Re Tapper's Estate, App.4 Dist., 432 So.2d 135 (Fla. 1983); Hulsh v. Hulsh, 431 So.2d 658 (App.1 Dist. Fla. 1983), review denied 440 So.2d 352; Flagship National Bank v. King, 418 So.2d 275 (App.3 Dist. Fla. 1982); Weintraub v. Weintraub, 417 So.2d 629 (Fla. 1982); Holland v. Holland, 406 So.2d 496 (App. Fla. 1981); Baker v. Baker, 394 So.2d 465 (App.4 Dist. Fla. 1981), petition denied 402 So.2d 607; De Garcia's Estate v. Garcia, 399 So.2d 486 (App. Fla. 1981); Topper v. Stewart, App., 388 So.2d 1270 (Fla. 1980); Estate of Roberts, 388 So.2d 216 (Fla. 1980); Belcher v. Belcher, 307 So.2d 918 (Fla. 1975); Posner v. Posner, 206 So.2d 416 (Fla. 1968), 233 So.2d 381 (Fla. 1970), reversed on other grounds at 257 So.2d 530 (Fla. 1972); Del Vecchio v. Del Vecchio, 143 So.2d 17 (Fla. 1962).

Georgia

1. *General comment:* Georgia allows individuals to generally waive marital rights and enter into "future settlements" under both written and oral agreements to be enforced during the life of the other spouse. Georgia law also refers to "marriage contracts" made in contemplation of marriage, which are required to be in writing and attested by two witnesses.

Best practice is to reduce all such agreements to writing.

2. *Divorce contingency provision allowed?* Yes. Georgia is one of the states which overruled prior state law in embracing the modern trend and rationale in this area. Where such agreement exists, however, the court will examine to determine whether there has been fraud, error, mistake, or changed circumstances making the PREMA unfair and unreasonable, and whether the overall impact is unconscionable.

3. *Common-law marriage state?* Yes.

4. *Community property state?* No.

5. *Legal authorities and references:* Official Code of Georgia, Article 3, Sections 19-3-60–65; Scherer v. Scherer, 249 Ga. 635, 292 S.E.2d 662 (1982); Wilcox v. Wilcox, 225 Ga. 472, 169 S.E.2d 819 (1969); Lowe v. Bryant, 30 Ga. 528 (1860).

Hawaii

1. *General comment:* Hawaii has adopted the general waiver provisions of the Uniform Probate Code, which allow couples to waive marital rights in writing after fair disclosure.

Hawaii has very little case law on point.

2. *Divorce contingency provision allowed?* Unknown.

3. *Common-law marriage state?* No.

4. *Community property state?* No.

5. *Legal authorities and references:* Hawaii Revised Statutes, Section 560:2-204; Long v. Pfluger, 6 Haw. 72 (1872).

Idaho

1. *General comment:* Marriage settlements contrary to the general statutory scheme of things are allowed in Idaho if they are in writing and are acknowledged or proved in the same manner as conveyances of land. When real estate is involved, the marriage settlement agreement must be recorded in every county in which the real estate affected by the agreement is located. If the agreement is not recorded, it has "like effect as the . . . nonrecording of a conveyance of real property." As a practical matter, then, it is believed that a nonrecorded agreement would still be effective *as between the parties themselves,* but the rights of outside parties may intervene.

Safe practice would thus call for acknowledgment by a notary public and later recording, especially if real estate is involved.

2. *Divorce contingency provision allowed?* Unknown.
3. *Common-law marriage state?* Yes.
4. *Community property state?* Yes.
5. *Legal authorities and references:* Idaho Code, Sections 32-916 to 32-920; Suchan v. Suchan, 682 P.2d 607 (Idaho 1984); Stockdale v. Stockdale, 102 Idaho, 643 P.2d 82 (Ct.App. 1982).

Illinois

1. *General comment:* Illinois recognizes the validity of written premarital agreements which comply with the general rules relating to fairness and disclosure applied throughout the jurisdictions.
2. *Divorce contingency provision allowed?* Yes, but only if the provision is fair and reasonable. The Illinois Appellate Court has specifically disapproved, for example, a provision which relieves a spouse of the duty of support while the parties are still married but separated prior to the entry of a decree of dissolution of marriage.
3. *Common-law marriage state?* No.
4. *Community property state?* No.
5. *Legal authorities and references:* Dubin v. Wise, 41 Ill.App.3d 132, 354 N.E.2d 403 (1976); Eule v. Eule, 24 Ill.App.3d 83, 320 N.E.2d 506 (1974); Volid v. Volid, 6 Ill.App.3d 386, 286 N.E.2d 42 (1974); Lee v. Central National Bank & Trust Co. of Rockford, 56 Ill.2d 394, 308 N.E.2d 605, 81 A.L.R.3d 444 (1974); Re Cullen's Estate, 66 Ill.App.2d 217, 213 N.E.2d 8 (1965); Van Cura v. Drangelis, 43 Ill.App.2d 205, 193 N.E.2d 201 (1963); Guhl v. Guhl, 376 Ill. 100, 33 N.E.2d 185 (1941); Kohler v. Kohler, 316 Ill. 33, 146 N.E. 476 (1925); Murdock v. Murdock, 219 Ill. 123, 76 N.E. 57 (1905); Taylor v. Taylor, 144 Ill. 436, 33 N.E. 532 (1893).

Indiana

1. *General comment:* In 1953 Indiana adopted the waiver provisions of the Model Probate Code at the time. The Indiana Code has separate waiver sections for an intestate estate (without a will) and for an election to take against a will—and the language is somewhat different regarding whether "full disclosure" is required for validity in each case. The safe practice is to give full disclosure in Indiana.

The Indiana Code provides that the waiver agreement "may be filed" in the same manner as the filing of an election to take against a will. It is unclear what would happen if it is not filed in the same way as such an election. To be safe, then, the PREMA should be filed with the probate clerk after the death of the spouse. A telephone call to the clerk of court at your local courthouse will tell you what the time limitations are at the time of your spouse's death.

2. *Divorce contingency provision allowed?* Yes, but case law indicates that use of any such provision will be restricted. For example, in allowing enforcement of a PREMA provision that stated that in the event of a divorce the wife would not ask for or receive from the husband any part of his property, the court noted that the agreement did not absolve the husband from alimony or place a maximum limitation on the wife's right to property distribution.

Thus, the future position of the Indiana court is uncertain, but in allowing a limited divorce contingency provision in 1976 it made the point that in the case in question they "need not go as far" as the courts in some of the other states in this area of the law. More recent cases have disclosed a continued cautious favoring of premarital agreements, but in the realm of divorce contingency provisions one must proceed with great care.

3. *Common-law marriage state?* No.

4. *Community property state?* No.

5. *Legal authorities and references:* Indiana Code, Sections 29-1-2-13 and 29-1-3-6; Russell v. Walz, 458 N.E.2d 1172 (Ind.App.3 Dist. 1984); Bohnke v. Estate of Bohnke, 454 N.E.2d 446 (Ind.App.4 Dist. 1983); Eagleson v. Viets, 443 N.E.2d 343 (Ind.App. 1982); Gillian's Estate v. Gillian's Estate, 406 N.E.2d 981 (Ind.App. 1980); Tomlinson v. Tomlinson, 170 Ind.App. 331, 352 N.E.2d 785 (1976); McClain's Estate v. McClain, 183 N.E.2d 182 (Ind. 1962); Baugher v. Barrett, 128 Ind.App. 233, 145 N.E.2d 297 (1957); Wheelock v. Wheelock, 97 Ind.App. 501, 187 N.E. 205 (1933); Leach v. Rains, 149 Ind. 152, 48 N.E. 858 (1897); Blake v. Blake, 15 Ind.App. 492, 44 N.E. 488 (1896).

Iowa

1. *General comment:* Iowa recognizes the validity of PREMAs which are fairly, freely, and understandingly entered into after full and free disclosure.

2. *Divorce contingency provision allowed?* A provision in a PREMA which on its face prohibits alimony or property settlement in the event of divorce is void as contrary to public policy (though the divorce chapter of the Iowa Code acknowledges that the provi-

sions of a PREMA shall be a factor to be "considered" by the court in determining property settlements, alimony, and the like).

The language of the *Norris* case, below, is often cited as a classic example of the reasoning used by the courts in refusing to allow divorce contingency provisions: "[T]he state interest in preserving the marriage relationship makes any provision which provides for, facilitates or tends to induce a separation or divorce of the parties after marriage contrary to public policy and void" (pp. 369–70 of 174 N.W.2d).

3. *Common-law marriage state?* Yes.

4. *Community property state?* No.

5. *Legal authorities and references:* Iowa Code, Sections 598.21(1)-(1) and 598.21(2)(i); Coffman v. Adkins, 338 N.W.2d 540 (Iowa App. 1983); In Re Marriage of Winegard, 278 N.W.2d 505 (Iowa 1979), cert. denied Winegard v. Calvin, 100 S.Ct. 425, 44 U.S. 951, 62 L.Ed.2d 321; In Re Gudenkauf's Marriage, 204 N.W.2d 586 (Iowa 1973); Norris v. Norris, 174 N.W.2d 368 (Iowa 1970); Christians v. Christians, 241 Iowa 1017, 44 N.W.2d 431 (1950); O'Dell v. O'Dell, 26 N.W.2d 401 (Iowa 1947).

Kansas

1. *General comment:* Kansas has long recognized the validity of "marriage settlements or contracts." The statutory recognition of PREMAs is mostly stated in the negative, by providing that "[n]othing in [the Domestic Relations Act] shall invalidate any marriage settlement or contract now made or hereafter made." General rules regarding fairness and disclosure apply.

2. *Divorce contingency provision allowed?* The Kansas court has stricken down divorce contingency provisions because they were unfair and in general void as against public policy. It is noteworthy that the cases coming before the Kansas Supreme Court have involved manifestly unfair factual situations or outright shams. Whether the court would take a different position when presented with a set of fair provisions is of course unknown. Therefore it would be dangerous at this time to rely on a divorce contingency provision in Kansas.

3. *Common-law marriage state?* Yes.

4. *Community property state?* No.

5. *Legal authorities and references:* Kansas Revised Statutes, Section 23-207; Ranney v. Ranney, 219 Kan. 428, 548 P.2d 734 (1976); In

Re Estate Of Taylor, 205 Kan. 347, 469 P.2d 437 (1970); In Re Estate of Johnson, 202 Kan. 684, 452 P.2d 301 (1969); Bremer v. Bremer, 187 Kan. 225, 356 P.2d 672 (1960); In Re Ward's Estate, 178 Kan. 366, 285 P.2d 1081 (1955); Fincham v. Fincham, 160 Kan. 683, 165 P.2d 209 (1946); In Re Garden's Estate, 158 Kan. 554, 148 P.2d 745 (1944); Pattison v. Pattison, 129 Kan. 558, 283 P. 483 (1930); Watson v. Watson, 104 Kan. 578, 180 P. 242, 182 P. 643 (1919), modified on rehearing 106 Kan. 693, 189 P. 949, rehearing denied 107 Kan. 193, 191 P. 482.

Kentucky

1. *General comment:* Kentucky recognizes written PREMAs if there is no fraud, deception, misrepresentation, concealment or undue influence.

2. *Divorce contingency provision allowed?* The Kentucky Supreme Court has stricken down PREMA provisions which provide for future divorce or separation as being void as against public policy. The court has recently noted that its position is part of a long-standing precedent, but it has stated that the position should be strictly read so as to keep it within reasonable bounds.

The court has hinted that, if the proper case were presented, it might reconsider its long-standing rule. At present, though, it would be dangerous to include a divorce contingency provision in a Kentucky PREMA.

3. *Common-law marriage state?* No.

4. *Community property state?* No.

5. *Legal authorities and references:* Kentucky Revised Statutes, Section 392.020; Jackson v. Jackson, 626 S.W.2d 630 (Ky. 1981); Sousley v. Sousley, 614 S.W.2d 942 (Ky. 1981); Brown v. Brown, 265 S.W.2d 484 (1954); Martin v. Martin, 282 Ky. 411, 138 S.W.2d 509 (1940); Wigginton v. Leech's Adm'x, 285 Ky. 787, 149 S.W.2d 531 (1941); Campbell v. Campbell, 377 S.W.2d 93 (Ky.Ct.App. 1964); Anderson v. Anderson, 194 Ky. 763, 240 S.W. 1061 (1922); Gaines v. Gaines' Adm'r, 163 Ky. 260, 173 S.W. 744 (1915); Jones Adm'r v. Jones Adm'r, 280 Ky. 37, 132 S.W.2d 509 (1939); Hardesty v. Hardesty's Ex'or., 236 Ky. 809, 34 S.W.2d 402 (1930); Stratton v. Wilson, 170 Ky. 61, 185 S.W. 522 (1916); Maze's Executor v. Maze, 30 Ky. LR 679, 99 S.W. 336 (1907).

Louisiana

1. *General comment:* Louisiana allows parties, by "matrimonial agreement," to modify or terminate the "legal regime" regarding matrimonial property. "Legal regime" is defined as the "community of acquets and gains" established under the Louisiana Civil Code. The matrimonial agreement must not be contrary to public policy. No court approval is required if the parties enter into it before marriage. After marriage, though, they may modify or terminate the matrimonial regime only upon filing a joint petition to the court and a finding by the court that the POSTMA serves their best interests and that they understand the nature of the agreement. If, after previously opting out of the matrimonial regime, the parties wish to subject themselves to it they may do so without court approval.

During the first year after moving into and acquiring a domicile in Louisiana spouses may enter into a matrimonial agreement without court approval.

Unless fully emancipated, a minor may not enter into a matrimonial agreement without the written concurrence of the father and mother, or guardian or tutor of the person.

Under the Louisiana Civil Code a creditor may sue to annul a matrimonial agreement in defraud of his rights.

Though not directly concerned with PREMAs, the Louisiana law protecting "forced heirs," such as children, should be taken into consideration in estate planning in the state.

2. *Divorce contingency provision allowed?* The Louisiana Supreme Court has held void a PREMA provision in which a wife waived her right to alimony pendente lite (marital support during litigation) in an action for judicial separation, as being contrary to public policy. The court did not state what its position was regarding divorce contingency provisions in general, or regarding *permanent* alimony in particular. Louisiana's position regarding *property settlement provisions* contingent on divorce was not stated.

3. *Common law marriage state?* No.

4. *Community property state?* Yes.

5. *Legal authorities and references:* Louisiana Civil Code, Articles 1734-1755, 2327-2333; Heyl v. Heyl, 445 So.2d 88 (App.2 Cir. La. 1984), writ denied 446 So.2d 1228; Brumfield v. Brumfield, 415 So.2d 520 (La.App. 1982); Rittiner v. Sinclair, 374 So.2d 680 (La.App. 1978); Holliday v. Holliday, 358 So.2d 618 (La. 1978); Flores v. Lemee, 16

La. 271 (1840); 39 La. Law Rev. 1161 (1979); 43 La. Law Rev. 159 (1982).

Maine

1. *General comment:* Maine allows "marriage settlements or contracts" which comply with the general principles applicable to PREMAs throughout the jurisdictions.
2. *Divorce contingency provision allowed?* Unknown.
3. *Common-law marriage state?* No.
4. *Community property state?* No.
5. *Legal authorities and references:* Maine Revised Statutes, Section 585; Wilson v. Wilson, 170 A.2d 679 (Me. 1961); Busque v. Marcov, 86 A.2d 873, 30 A.L.R.2d 1411 (1952); Rolfe v. Rolfe, 125 Me. 82, 130 A. 877 (1925); Denison v. Dawes, 121 Me. 402, 117 A. 314 (1922); Bright v. Chapman, 108 Me. 62, 72 A. 750 (1908); Tolman v. Ward, 86 Me. 303, 29 A. 1081 (1894).

Maryland

1. *General comment:* Maryland allows PREMAs which do not tend to induce divorce and in which there has been frank, full, and truthful disclosure. The Maryland high court states that a confidential relationship exists between parties about to be married.
2. *Divorce contingency provision allowed?* Recently the Maryland Court of Appeals has held that PREMAs which settle property rights or alimony upon divorce "are not per se against public policy." This position in effect rejected language to the contrary in earlier case law. It thus appears that Maryland residents can now proceed cautiously with a divorce contingency provision.
3. *Common-law marriage state?* No.
4. *Community property state?* No.
5. *Legal authorities and references:* Code of Maryland, Sections 3-205, 8-101 and 8-103; Frey v. Frey, 298 Md. 552, 471 A.2d 705 (1984); Goldberg v. Goldberg, 290 Md. 204, 428 A.2d 469 (1981); Hartz v. Hartz, 248 Md. 47, 234 A.2d 865 (1967); Cohn v. Cohn, 209 Md. 470, 121 A.2d 704 (1956) (partially rejected in the *Frey* case above); Ortel v. Gettig, 207 Md. 594, 116 A.2d 145 (1955); Levy v. Sherman, 185 Md. 63, 43 A.2d 25 (1945); Busey v. McCurley, 61 Md. 436 (1884).

Massachusetts

1. *General comment:* Massachusetts recognizes the validity of PREMAs under the general principles of fairness and disclosure adhered to throughout the jurisdictions. After January 3, 1979, the "Wellington rule"—which negates any requirement of disclosure of worth—was done away with. For PREMAs executed after that date there is the requirement of mutual disclosure, and in judging the validity of the agreement the courts will consider closely the degree of fairness and extent of disclosure of worth of the parties.

Massachusetts is one of the few jurisdictions which provides for recording PREMAs, stating that a schedule clearly defining the property affected by the PREMA shall be attached to the document, and shall be recorded with the registry of deeds or district where the husband resides, either before or within 90 days after the marriage. If the husband was not a resident before the marriage, the recording should be in the registry of deeds or district where the wife resides at the time of the marriage.

If the PREMA is not recorded it is void *except* as between the parties thereto, their heirs and personal representatives. Stated otherwise, it is not necessary for the couple to record the PREMA to make it effective *as between themselves.*

2. *Divorce contingency provision allowed?* Yes, although the Massachusetts Supreme Judicial Court insists that the divorce-related provisions be fair at the time of signing *and* that they be fair under the circumstances existing at the time of enforcement. An example of unfairness: if enforcement of the PREMA would result in one spouse becoming a "public charge" while the other owned sufficient assets to reasonably prevent such an occurrence.

3. *Common law marriage state?* No.

4. *Community property state?* No.

5. *Legal authorities and references:* Massachusetts General Laws, Chapter 209, Sections 25–27; Osborne v. Osborne, 384 Mass. 591, 428 N.E.2d 810 (Mass. 1981); Rosenberg v. Lipnick, 377 Mass. 666, 389 N.E.2d 385 (Mass. 1979); Whitney v. Buck, 3 Mass.App. 766, 330 N.E.2d 213 (Mass. 1975); Price v. Price, 341 Mass. 390, 170 N.E.2d 346 (Mass. 1960); Wellington v. Rugg, 243 Mass. 30, 136 N.E. 831 (1922); 70 Mass.L.Rev. 82 (1985); 25 Boston Bar J. No 5, p.7; 50 Mass.L.Q. No.2, p.157; 48 Mass.L.Q. 303.

Michigan

1. *General comment:* Michigan allows PREMAs which conform to the general requirements of fairness, disclosure and lack of fraud recognized throughout the jurisdictions.

If the woman is under age when signing the document she shall be joined in it by her father or guardian.

2. *Divorce contingency provision allowed?* Michigan takes the general position that any marriage agreement provision that provides for or seeks to effectuate a future separation or divorce is invalid. Thus extreme caution is called for.

3. *Common-law marriage state?* No.

4. *Community property state?* No.

5. *Legal authorities and references:* Michigan Compiled Laws, Sections 558.14–16; 702.74a; 722.53; Re Estate of Benker, 416 Mich. 681, 331 N.W.2d 193 (1982); Rockwell v. Rockwell's Estate, 24 Mich.App. 593, 180 N.W.2d 498 (1970); M & D Robinson Co. v. Dunitz, 12 Mich. App. 5, 162 N.W.2d 318 (Mich. 1968); In Re Muxlow's Estate, 367 Mich. 133, 116 N.W.2d 43 (1962); Granger v. Granger, 296 Mich. 357, 296 N.W. 288 (Mich. 1941); Hockenberry v. Donovan, 170 Mich. 370, 136 N.W. 389 (Mich. 1912); In Re Pulling's Estate, 93 Mich. 274, 52 N.W. 1116 (Mich. 1892); Pulling v. Durfee, 85 Mich. 3, 48 N.W. 48, 41 Mich.L.Rev. 1133 (1943).

Minnesota

1. *General comment:* Minnesota has one of the more comprehensive statutes dealing with premarital agreements. A PREMA will be considered valid and enforceable if there is a full and fair disclosure of both the *earnings* and property of the parties, and the parties have had the opportunity to consult with legal counsel of their own choice.

Procedurally under Minnesota law a PREMA should be in writing, executed in the presence of two witnesses, and acknowledged before a notary public or other person authorized to administer an oath in the state, and should be signed before the day of the marriage. If the PREMA affects legally described real estate, it "may" be recorded or filed with the county recorder of every county where the real estate is situated. A failure to record does not seem to affect the validity of the PREMA *as between the parties,* but shall render the document void as against subsequent good-faith purchasers, lawful attachments and judgment holders.

State Laws

2. *Divorce contingency provision allowed?* Yes, by statute. The law specifically allows a divorce contingency provision regarding the *nonmarital,* or separate, property owned by the parties, and it also declares that a PREMA covering *marital* property is allowable if it is valid and enforceable otherwise under Minnesota law.

The Minnesota statute speaks in terms of rights in *property,* and there has been no indication since the enactment of its law in 1979 what the Minnesota position would be if there were an attempt to prohibit or limit *alimony* in the event of divorce.

3. *Common-law marriage state?* No.

4. *Community property state?* No.

5. *Legal authorities and references:* Minnesota Statutes, Section 519.11; Serbus' Estate v. Serbus, 324 N.W.2d 381 (Minn. 1982); Hafner v. Hafner, 295 N.W.2d 567 (Minn. 1980); Englund v. Englund, 286 Minn. 227, 175 N.W.2d 461 (1970); Gartner v. Gartner, 74 N.W.2d 809 (Minn. 1956); O'Brien v. Lien, 160 Minn. 276, 199 N.W. 914 (1924); Welsh v. Welsh, 150 Minn. 23, 184 N.W. 38 (1921); Haraldson v. Knutson, 142 Minn. 109, 171 N.W. 201 (1919); Slingerland v. Slingerland, 115 Minn. 270, 132 N.W. 326 (1911); 51 Hennepin Lawyer 6 (Sept.–Oct. 1981).

Mississippi

1. *General comment:* Mississippi appears to allow PREMAs under the general rules pertaining to fairness and disclosure recognized throughout the jurisdictions.

Mississippi has limited case law on point.

2. *Divorce contingency provision allowed?* Unknown.

3. *Common-law marriage state?* No.

4. *Community property state?* No.

5. *Legal authorities and references:* Roberts v. Roberts, 381 So.2d 1333 (Miss. 1980); Watson v. Duncan, 84 Miss. 763, 34 So. 125 (1904); Stevenson v. Renardet, 83 Miss. 382, 35 So. 576 (1904); Rothschild v. Hatch, 54 Miss. 554 (1877); Wiley v. Gray, 36 Miss. 510 (1858); Williams v. Claiborne, 7 Smedes & M. 488 (Miss. 1846).

Missouri

1. *General comment:* Missouri recognizes the validity of express PREMAs, holding that the ultimate question involves whether the spouse against whom the agreement is sought to be enforced "has

129

been defrauded or overreached." Full disclosure and fair consideration also must be shown.

2. *Divorce contingency provision allowed?* Yes, but "only if the
provisions are conscionable and if the agreement was fairly made."
In the case in which the Missouri Court of Appeals made the quoted
statement that it would allow such divorce contingency provisions,
it went on to find that the waiver of all property rights and alimony
was invalid because it was basically unfair and possibly even unconscionable under those particular facts.

3. *Common-law marriage state?* No.

4. *Community property state?* No.

5. *Legal authorities and references:* Missouri Statutes, Section 474.-
120; Ludwig v. Ludwig, 693 S.W.2d 816 (Mo.App. 1985); Roberts v.
Estate of Roberts, 664 S.W.2d 634 (Mo.App. 1984); Estate of Murphy,
661 S.W.2d 657 (Mo.App. 1983); Hosmer v. Hosmer, 611 S.W.2d 32
(Mo.App. 1980); Ferry v. Ferry, 286 S.W.2d 782 (Mo.App. 1979); In
Re Adelman's Estate, 377 S.W.2d 549 (Mo.App. 1964); Quint v. Quint,
359 S.W.2d 29 (Mo.App. 1962); Chapman v. Corbin, 316 S.W.2d 880
(Mo.App. 1958); Broyles v. Magee, 71 S.W.2d 149 (Mo.App. 1934);
Vogel v. Vogel, 22 Mo. 161 (1855); 46 Mo. Law Rev. 228 (1981);
UMKC L.Rev. 31 (1978).

Montana

1. *General comment:* Montana has adopted the general waiver
provisions of the Uniform Probate Code, thus allowing the parties to
waive, in writing, all marital rights after fair disclosure.

There is very little case law on point.

2. *Divorce contingency provision allowed?* Unknown.

3. *Common-law marriage state?* Yes.

4. *Community property state?* No.

5. *Legal authorities and references:* Revised Code of Montana, Section 72-2-102; Stefonick v. Stefonick, 167 P.2d. 848 (Mont. 1948); Re
Oppenheimer's Estate, 73 Mont. 560, 238 P. 599 (1925).

Nebraska

1. *General comment:* Nebraska has adopted the general waiver
provisions of the Uniform Probate Code, thus allowing the parties to
waive all marital rights in writing after fair disclosure.

2. *Divorce contingency provision allowed?* No. When presented

with the opportunity to join the modern trend in this area the Nebraska Supreme Court in a 1982 case declined to do so, holding that divorce contingency provisions tend to promote divorce and are therefore void as being contrary to public policy.

3. *Common-law marriage state?* No.

4. *Community property state?* No.

5. *Legal authorities and references:* Revised Statutes of Nebraska, Sections 30-2316 and 42-204, 42-205; Mulford v. Mulford, 211 Neb. 747, 320 N.W.2d 470 (1982); In Re Moss' Estate, 200 Neb. 215, 263 N.W.2d 98 (1978); In Re Strickland's Estate, 181 Neb. 478, 149 N.W.2d 344 (1967); Bassett v. First National Bank & Trust Co., 189 Neb. 206, 201 N.W.2d 848 (1972); Re Spieth Estate, 181 Neb. 11, 146 N.W.2d 746 (1966); Re Dorshorst's Estate, 174 Neb. 886, 120 N.W.2d 32 (1963); Wulf v. Wulf, 129 Neb. 808, 263 N.W. 222 (1935); Stahl v. Stahl, 115 Neb. 582, 215 N.W. 131 (1927); Tiernan v. Tiernan, 112 Neb. 707, 201 N.W. 145 (1924).

Nevada

1. *General comment:* Nevada allows PREMAs under the general rules relating to fairness and disclosure recognized throughout the jurisdictions. In Nevada all "marriage contracts or settlements" must be in writing and executed, acknowledged, or proved in like manner as a conveyance of land. They must be recorded with the Recorder in every county in which real estate affected by the document is situated. If not so recorded the agreement is not valid as to the real estate affected thereby, except the agreement shall nonetheless be effective *as to the parties to the agreement.*

Thus, as noted elsewhere in this book, an unrecorded "marriage contract or settlement" under such a law is fully valid and enforceable *as between the parties to the document.*

2. *Divorce contingency provision allowed?* Yes, if it is not obtained by fraud, misrepresentation, material disclosure, or duress, and if the overall result is not unconscionable.

3. *Common-law marriage state?* No.

4. *Community property state?* Yes.

5. *Legal authorities and references:* Nevada Revised Statutes, Sections 123.270–300; Buetter v. Buetter, 505 P.2d 600 (Nev. 1973).

New Hampshire

1. *General comment:* New Hampshire allows PREMAs under the general rules relating to fairness and disclosure applicable throughout the jurisdictions. New Hampshire law specifically provides that such marriage "settlements" are enforceable by the court of probate.
2. *Divorce contingency provision allowed?* Unclear.
3. *Common-law marriage state?* No.
4. *Community property state?* No.
5. *Legal authorities and references:* New Hampshire Revised Statutes, Sections 560:15–16; Hanke v. Hanke, 123 N.H. 175, 459 A.2d 246 (1983); In Re Estate of Wood, 122 N.H. 956, 453 A.2d 1251 (1982); Heald's Petition, 22 N.H. 265 (1851).

New Jersey

1. *General comment:* New Jersey allows PREMAs under the general rules relating to fairness and disclosure applicable throughout the jurisdictions. New Jersey case law refers to a requirement of disclosure of income as well as assets, and further superimposes a requirement that even if there has been full disclosure, the agreement cannot be "unconscionable."

New Jersey's one-sentence statute recognizing contracts made in contemplation of marriage is almost identical with a law that has been in existence in New York for many years.

The New Jersey legislature has before it a bill to adopt the substance of the Uniform Premarital Agreement Act, and the law may become effective by the time this book reaches print. The Uniform Premarital Agreement Act has been discussed in the body of the book, and the language of the Uniform Act is set forth verbatim in Appendix 3 beginning on page 145.

2. *Divorce contingency provision allowed?* The New Jersey court has stated in a rather recent case that such a provision is enforceable if there has been full disclosure and if the agreement is not unconscionable. In a 1984 case the New Jersey court struck down such a PREMA provision in spite of the fact that the woman had had independent legal counsel and some disclosure had been made. In that case the man had assets of at least $5 million, annual income of $250,000, and the divorce contingency provision provided that she would have received a total of $100,000 if the marriage did not succeed.

Of course if the Uniform Act is adopted, such a provision would be authorized. Depending on the exact language of the legislation, the court may or may not still become involved if the agreement is "unconscionable".

3. *Common-law marriage state?* No.

4. *Community property state?* No.

5. *Legal authorities and references:* New Jersey Statutes, Section 37:2-4; Marschall v. Marschall, 195 N.J.Super. 16, 477 A.2d 833 (Ch.1984); Fern v. Fern, 140 N.J.Super. 121, 355 A.2d 672 (A.D.1976); Lomonaco v. Goodwin, 108 N.J.Super. 83, 260 A.2d 10 (Ch.1969); Herr v. Herr, 13 N.J. 79, 98 A.2d 55 (1953); First National Bank of Princeton v. Miley, 3 N.J.Super. 348, 65 A.2d 553 (1949); Kelso v. Kelso, 95 N.J.Eq. 544, 123 A. 250 (1924), affirmed 96 N.J.Eq. 354, 124 A. 763; Russell v. Russell, 60 N.J.Eq. 282, 47 A. 37 (1900), affirmed 63 N.J.Eq. 282, 49 A. 1081; 12 Rutgers L.J. 283 (1980); 3 Rutgers-Camden L.J. 175 (1971).

New Mexico

1. *General comment:* New Mexico recognizes the validity of PREMAs under the general rules, but specifically requires that the document be in writing and executed and acknowledged or proved in like manner as a grant of land is required to be executed and acknowledged or proved. The document must be recorded in the Recorder's office of every county in which any real estate may be situated which is granted or affected by such contract.

New Mexico law provides that a husband and wife cannot by contract "alter their legal relations, except of their property." This seems to set forth the general rule that the parties cannot contract away those basic things inherent in a normal marriage.

The New Mexico law was adopted from the old (pre-1985) California law.

2. *Divorce contingency provision allowed?* Unknown.

3. *Common-law marriage state?* No.

4. *Community property state?* Yes.

5. *Legal authorities and references:* New Mexico Statutes, Sections 40-2-4 to 40-2-9; Hurley v. Hurley, 94 N.M. 641, 615 P.2d 256 (1980); Tellez v. Tellez, 51 N.M. 416, 186 P.2d 390 (1947); Miller v. Miller, 33 N.M. 132, 262 P. 1007 (1928); Girard v. Girard, 29 N.M. 189, 221 P. 801 (1923).

New York

1. *General comment:* New York recognizes the validity of written PREMAs under the general rules relating to fairness and disclosure applicable throughout the jurisdictions.

2. *Divorce contingency provision allowed?* The full extent of a restrictive divorce contingency provision is unknown, but the New York courts have stricken down provisions which totally relieve a husband of alimony obligations in certain circumstances.

3. *Common-law marriage state?* No.

4. *Community property state?* No.

5. *Legal authorities and references:* New York General Obligations Law, Sections 3-303 and 5-701; Re Estate of Crawford, 115 Misc.2d 395, 454 N.Y.S.2d 258 (1982); Re Estate of Duckman, 110 Misc.2d 575, 442 N.Y.S.2d 909 (1981); Mitchell v. Mitchell, 310 A.2d 837 (C.A.D.C. 1973); In Re Matter of Sunshine, 40 N.Y.S.2d 875 (1976); Matter of Liberman, 6 Misc.2d 396, 162 N.Y.S.2d 62 (1957), 4 App. Div.2d 512, 167 N.Y.S.2d 158 (1957), affirmed 5 N.Y.2d 719, 152 N.E.2d 665 (1958); Benjamin v. Benjamin, 197 Misc. 618, 95 N.Y.S.2d 167 (1950), affirmed 277 AD 752, 97 N.Y.S.2d 196, affirmed 302 N.Y. 560, 96 N.E.2d 618; In Re Weeks' Will, 294 N.Y. 616, 63 N.E.2d 85 (1945); Mirizio v. Mirizio, 242 N.Y. 74, 150 N.E. 65 (1926); Van Deventer v. Van Deventer, 32 AD 578, 53 N.Y.S. 236 (1898); Spertell v. Hendrix, 93 App.Div.2d 788, 461 N.Y.S.2d 823 (1983, 1st Dept.) (involving unmarried cohabiting couple).

North Carolina

1. *General comment:* North Carolina allows "any persons of full age about to be married" to enter into valid marriage contracts if they are "not inconsistent with public policy." Such contracts, whether pre- or postmarital, may be entered into "with or without a valuable consideration." Despite such language, though, care must be taken to avoid fraud, overreaching, and lack of fair disclosure.

No POSTMA shall be valid to affect any real estate of the parties, or real estate income, for longer than three years after the POSTMA is made, "unless it is in writing and acknowledged by both parties before a certifying officer" (i.e., notary public, justice, judge, magistrate, clerk, assistant clerk or deputy clerk of the General Court of Justice, or the equivalent officers of the jurisdiction where the acknowledgment is made).

2. *Divorce contingency provision allowed?* Uncertain.
3. *Common-law marriage state?* No.
4. *Community property state?* No.
5. *Legal authorities and references:* North Carolina General Statutes, Section 52-10; Gray v. Snyder, 704 F.2d 709 (4th Cir. 1983); In Re Estate of Loftin, 285 N.C. 717, 208 S.E.2d 670 (1974); Motley v. Motley, 255 N.C. 190, 120 S.E.2d 422 (1961); Turner v. Turner, 242 N.C. 533, 89 S.E.2d 245 (1955); 47 N.C.L.Rev. 815 (1969).

North Dakota

1. *General comment:* North Dakota has adopted the general waiver provisions of the Uniform Probate Code, which allow couples to waive marital rights in writing after fair disclosure.

Also, North Dakota has now adopted the substance of the Uniform Premarital Agreement Act. (See Appendix 3 for the text of the Act.)

2. *Divorce contingency provision allowed?* Yes.
3. *Common-law marriage state?* No.
4. *Community property state?* No.
5. *Legal authorities and references:* North Dakota Century Code, Section 30.1-05-04 (2-204); Bender v. Bender, 64 N.D. 740, 256 N.W. 222 (1934); Charlson v. Charlson, 48 N.D. 851, 187 N.W. 418 (1922); Herr v. Herr, 45 N.D. 492, 178 N.W. 443 (1920); Swingle v. Swingle, 36 N.D. 611, 162 N.W. 912 (1917). (Any case law prior to enactment of the Uniform Premarital Agreement Act must now be read in the context of the new Act.)

Ohio

1. *General comment:* Ohio recognizes the validity of PREMAs under the general rules pertaining to fairness and disclosure applicable throughout the jurisdictions.

2. *Divorce contingency provision allowed?* Recent Ohio case law indicates that such provisions are not contrary to public policy. Other case law indicates that equitable principles would have to be closely adhered to, though.

3. *Common-law marriage state?* Yes.
4. *Community property state?* No.
5. *Legal authorities and references:* Ohio Revised Code, Sections 3103.05 and 3103.06; Gross v. Gross, 11 O.S.3d 99, 11 O.B.R. 400, 464 N.E.2d 500 (1984); Davis v. Davis, 258 N.E.2d 277 (Ohio 1970); Haw-

kins v. Hawkins, 185 N.E.2d 89 (Ohio 1962); Rocker v. Rocker, 13 Ohio Misc. 199, 232 N.E.2d 445 (1967); In Re Mosier's Estate, 133 N.E.2d 202 (Ohio 1954); 10 O.North L.Rev. 11 (1983); 53 O.Bar 463 (1980).

Oklahoma

1. *General comment:* Oklahoma recognizes the validity of PREMAs under the general rules relating to fairness and disclosure applied throughout the jurisdictions.

A recent Oklahoma case has restated the general rule upholding the validity of waiver provisions if they are specific. In the same case, though, the Oklahoma Supreme Court has ruled that a supposed waiver of a widow's homestead rights was invalid because it lacked specificity.

2. *Divorce contingency provision allowed?* Yes. Oklahoma is usually cited as one of the "progressives" in this area. The Oklahoma Court of Appeals has noted that public policy should encourage PREMAs under certain circumstances, and that such a provision might actually *encourage* marriages in some instances (such as where older, previously married couples might otherwise be afraid to marry). The court nonetheless has stated the need for full, fair, and frank disclosure, or at least a fairly accurate knowledge of the other's financial worth. In determining whether PREMAs are valid, the court will judge them on a case-by-case basis.

3. *Common-law marriage state?* Yes.

4. *Community property state?* No.

5. *Legal authorities and references:* In Re Meyers, 709 P.2d 1044 (Okla. 1985), In Re Burgess' Estate, 646 P.2d 623 (Okla.Ct.App. 1982); Matter of Baggerley's Estate, 635 P.2d 1333 (Okla.Ct.App. 1981); Freeman v. Freeman, 565 P.2d 365 (Okla. 1977); Dean v. Jelsma, 316 P.2d 599 (Okla. 1957); cert. denied 355 U.S. 954, rehearing denied 356 U.S. 928; In Re Cobb's Estate, 305 P.2d 1028 (1957); Blasingame v. Gathright, 284 P.2d 431 (1955).

Oregon

1. *General comment:* Oregon recognizes the validity of PREMAs under the general rules relating to disclosure and fairness applied throughout the jurisdictions. Oregon case law often refers to whether the spouse to whom the agreement was proposed was given the opportunity to consult with his or her own legal counsel.

Although Oregon's statute only specifically authorizes PREMAs regarding "personal property," case law has held that the agreements may include real estate as well as personal property.

2. *Divorce contingency provision allowed?* Yes. An often-cited Oregon case has upheld a "divorce contingency" clause in a PREMA where there had been adequate financial disclosure and independent legal counseling. In so holding, the Oregon court overruled prior case law on point. The court took note that a provision stating that no alimony will be paid upon divorce will be upheld unless the spouse has no other reasonable source of support. The court further pointed out that if circumstances change, the court has the power to modify the decree.

3. *Common-law marriage state?* No.

4. *Community property state?* No.

5. *Legal authorities and references:* Oregon Revised Statutes, Section 108.140; In Re Marriage of Norris, 51 Or.App. 43, 624 P.2d 636 (1981); In Re Marriage of Coward, 35 Or.App. 677, 582 P.2d 834 (1978); Merrill v. Estate of Merrill, 275 Or. 653, 552 P.2d 249 (1976); In Re Marriage of Unander, 265 Or. 102, 506 P.2d 719 (1973); Bauer v. Bauer, 1 Or.App. 504, 464 P.2d 710 (1970); In Re Estate of Moore, 210 Or. 23, 307 P.2d 483 (1957); Newton v. Pickell, 269 P.2d 508 (Or. 1954).

Pennsylvania

1. *General comment:* Pennsylvania allows PREMAs if they are entered into freely, understandingly, without fraud, with adequate disclosure, and if the provisions for the spouse are reasonable. In evaluating the reasonableness of a PREMA provision for a spouse, such determination must be made as of the time of the agreement, and not by hindsight. In such determination the courts will compare the living standard of the contesting spouse before the marriage to the standard which might reasonably be expected during the marriage.

2. *Divorce contingency provision allowed?* Uncertain. The general public policy as expressed so often in the cases would suggest that much might depend on whether the much-cited "reasonableness" test has been met.

3. *Common-law marriage state?* Yes.

4. *Community property state?* No.

5. *Legal authorities and references:* Divorce Code of 1980, 23 P.S. Sections 101 and following; In Re Estate of Geyer, 338 Pa.Super. 157,

487 A.2d 901 (1985); Fox v. Fox, 31 D.& C.3d 30 (Pa.Comm.Pl. 1984); In Re Spott's Estate, 3 Fiduciary 419 (Pa.Comm.Pl. 1983); In Re Sweet's Estate, 25 D. & C.3d 357 (Pa.Comm.Pl. 1983); In Re Kester's Estate, 486 Pa. 349, 405 A.2d 1244 (1979); In Re Slight's Estate, 467 Pa. 619, 359 A.2d 773 (1976); In Re Ratony's Estate, 443 Pa. 454, 277 A.2d 792 (1971); In Re Perelman's Estate, 438 Pa. 112, 263 A.2d 375 (1970); In Re Vallish's Estate, 431 Pa. 88, 244 A.2d 745 (1968).

Rhode Island

1. *General comment:* There is little law on point, but Rhode Island appears to subscribe to the general rules allowing PREMAs throughout the jurisdictions.
2. *Divorce contingency provision allowed?* Unknown.
3. *Common-law marriage state?* Yes.
4. *Community property state?* No.
5. *Legal authorities and references:* Cole v. Cole, 21 A.2d 248, 67 R.I. 168, reargument denied 22 A.2d 337, 67 R.I. 168 (1941); Peck v. Peck, 12 R.I. 485, 34 Am.Rep. 702 (1880); Law v. Smith, 2 R.I. 244 (1852).

South Carolina

1. *General comment:* South Carolina allows PREMAs if they are voluntarily made, entered into in good faith, and are fair and equitable.
2. *Divorce contingency provision allowed?* Unknown.
3. *Common-law marriage state?* Yes.
4. *Community property state?* No.
5. *Legal authorities and references:* Code of Laws of South Carolina, Section 21-17-110; Stork v. First National Bank of South Carolina, 281 S.C. 515, 316 S.E.2d 400 (1984); South Carolina Loan & Trust Co. v. Lawton, 69 S.C. 345, 48 S.E. 282 (1904), Hatcher v. Robertson, 4 Strob.Eq. 179 (1850); Fripp v. Talbird, 1 Hill, Eq. 142 (1833).

South Dakota

1. *General comment:* South Dakota has adopted the general waiver provisions of the Uniform Probate Code, which allow a surviving spouse to waive marital rights in writing after fair disclosure.

2. *Divorce contingency provision allowed?* The South Dakota Supreme Court has stricken down, as contrary to public policy, PREMA provisions which attempt to limit alimony which would be payable to a spouse in the event of divorce or legal separation. The court has expressly embraced such a position in spite of "the trend of judicial decisions in other jurisdictions."

3. *Common-law marriage state?* No.

4. *Community property state?* No.

5. *Legal authorities and references:* South Dakota Codified Laws, Section 30-5A-4; Connolly v. Connolly, 270 N.W.2d 44 (S.D. 1978); Schutterle v. Schutterle, 260 N.W.2d 341 (S.D. 1977); In Re Buss' Estate, 71 S.D. 529, 26 N.W.2d 700 (1947).

Tennessee

1. *General comment:* Tennessee law provides that PREMAs are binding if the court determines that the agreement was entered into by the couple freely, knowledgeably and in good faith, and without exertion of duress or undue influence upon either spouse.

No PREMA shall be good against creditors when the document sets aside for the intended spouse or children an amount which is greater than such spouse would have received under the marriage and probate laws of Tennessee.

Tennessee law requires that marriage "contracts of settlement" should be registered in every county in which the wife's personal property or the real estate affected by the contract is situated. Such registration is required to protect against the husband's creditors, but is not required for validity of the contract as between the parties to the contract.

2. *Divorce contingency provision allowed?* Tennessee holds that a PREMA provision which attempts to limit alimony in the event of divorce is conducive to divorce and therefore void as against public policy.

3. *Common-law marriage state?* No.

4. *Community property state?* No.

5. *Legal authorities and references:* Tennessee Code, Sections 36-3-501, 36-3-502, 66-24-105, and 66-24-106; Duncan v. Duncan, 652 S.W.2d 913 (Tenn.Ct.App. 1983); Crouch v. Crouch, 385 S.W.2d 288 (Tenn. 1964); Key v. Collins, 145 Tenn. 106, 236 S.W. 3 (1921).

Texas

1. *General comment:* Texas allows PREMAs under the general principles recognized throughout the jurisdictions. Recent case law has referred to the validity of PREMAs where there has been no fraud or lack of understanding, and where there has been full disclosure of the nature and extent of the property interests involved.

A competent minor may enter into a PREMA only with the written, subscribed consent of the guardian of the minor's estate and with the approval of the probate court after the application, notice, and hearing required in the Probate Code for the sale of a minor's real estate. If there be no guardian of the minor's estate, the written, subscribed consent of the minor's managing conservator must be obtained.

2. *Divorce contingency provision allowed?* Unknown.

3. *Common-law marriage state?* Yes.

4. *Community property state?* Yes.

5. *Legal authorities and references:* Vernon's Texas Code Annotated, Section 5.41; Williams v. Williams, 569 S.W.2d 867 (Tex.Sup. 1978); Huff v. Huff, 554 S.W.2d 841 (Tex.Civ.App. 1977); Hayes v. Hayes, 378 S.W.2d 375 (Tex.Civ.App. 1964) (based on failure to witness a PREMA under a statute now repealed); Elmore v. State, 126 Cr.R. 519, 73 S.W.2d 107 (Tex. 1934); 13 St. Mary's L.J. 449 (1982); 56 Texas L.Rev. 861 (1978).

Utah

1. *General comment:* Utah has extremely little law on the book pertaining to PREMAs. The best course would be to follow the general rules outlined throughout this book.

2. *Divorce contingency provision allowed?* Unknown.

3. *Common-law marriage state?* No.

4. *Community property state?* No.

5. *Legal authorities and references:* Because of the scarcity of law in this area in Utah, one should follow the general guidelines of this book. Reference to the law of non-community-property sister states would also be helpful. A generally conservative approach would be safest.

Vermont

1. *General comment:* Vermont allows PREMAs under the general rules recognized throughout the jurisdictions. The Vermont Supreme

Court refers to the necessity that there be no fraud or unconscionable advantage taken at the time of execution of the PREMA.

2. *Divorce contingency provision allowed?* Full extent unknown.

3. *Common-law marriage state?* No.

4. *Community property state?* No.

5. *Legal authorities and references:* Legault v. Legault, 142 Vt. 525, 459 A.2d 980 (1983); Padova v. Padova, 123 Vt. 125, 183 A.2d 227 (1962); In Re Prudenzano's Will, 116 Vt. 55, 68 A.2d 704 (1949); Munsell v. Munsell's Estate, 95 Vt. 103, 113 A. 521 (1921); Mann v. Mann's Estate, 53 Vt. 48 (1880).

Virginia

1. *General comment:* Effective July 1, 1986, Virginia adopted the substance of the new Uniform Premarital Agreement Act. This gives Virginians many advantages in the areas of flexibility and certainty which are lacking in states which depend primarily in this field upon individual case-law interpretations. See Appendix 3 for the text of the Uniform Premarital Agreement Act.

Except for a few more minor differences, Virginia's main variance from the Uniform Act is that it does not contain the Uniform Act's provision that if the PREMA eliminates or modifies spousal support (i.e., alimony) to the extent that the spouse becomes eligible for public assistance, the court may require the other party to provide enough support to avoid that eligibility.

2. *Divorce contingency provision allowed?* Yes.

3. *Common-law marriage state?* No.

4. *Community property state?* No.

5. *Legal authorities and references:* Chapter 8 under Virginia's Domestic Relations, Sections 20-147 to 20-154; Bateman v. Rubin, 199 v. 156, 98 S.E.2d 519 (1957). (Any case law prior to enactment of the Virginia Premarital Agreement Act must now be read in the context of the new Act. All pre-Act PREMAs are stated to "be valid and enforceable if otherwise valid as contracts.")

Washington

1. *General comment:* Washington recognizes the validity of PREMAs under the general rules relating to fairness and disclosure applied throughout the jurisdictions. In scrutinizing PREMAs the Washington courts have referred to such factors as whether there has

been a full and fair disclosure of all material facts relating to amount, character, and value of the property to which claim will be waived. Some Washington case law also inquires whether the spouse has had independent legal counsel. Also, Washington has a statute which requires "good faith" in transactions between spouses.

2. *Divorce contingency provision allowed?* Unclear. The provisions of a PREMA have been used as the basis for property division in rather recent Washington case law. Whether such a provision would be allowed to achieve a result which is manifestly "unfair" under the Washington interpretations is doubtful.

3. *Common-law marriage state?* No.

4. *Community property state?* Yes.

5. *Legal authorities and references:* Washington Rev. Code, Sections 26.16.120 and 26.16.210; Whitney v. Seattle-First National Bank, 90 Wash.2d 105, 579 P.2d 937 (1978); In Re Marriage of Cohn, 18 Wash.App. 502, 569 P.2d 79 (1977); In Re Marriage of Hadley, 88 Wash.2d 649, 575 P.2d 790 (1977); Friedlander v. Friedlander, 80 Wash.2d 293, 494 P.2d 208 (1972); Hamlin v. Merlino, 44 Wash.2d 851, 272 P.2d 125 (1954); Clark v. Baker, 76 Wash. 110, 135 P. 1025 (1913); 54 Wash.L.Rev. 109 (1978).

West Virginia

1. *General comment:* West Virginia recognizes the validity of PREMAs under the general rules applicable throughout the jurisdictions.

2. *Divorce contingency provision allowed?* Yes, such provisions are presumed to be valid where the terms of the PREMA are understandable and the parties had the opportunity to consult with counsel. Courts will be aware of "unconscionability," however.

3. *Common-law marriage state?* No.

4. *Community property state?* No.

5. *Legal authorities and references:* Gant v. Gant, 329 S.E.2d 106 (W.Va. 1985).

Wisconsin

1. *General comment:* Wisconsin allows PREMAs under the general rules relating to disclosure and fairness applied throughout the jurisdictions.

2. *Divorce contingency provision allowed?* In the past such a provi-

sion has been held to be unenforceable as violative of public policy.

3. *Common-law marriage state?* No.

4. *Community property state?* Beginning in 1986 Wisconsin enacted a law which amounts to adoption of a community property law system in the state.

5. *Legal authorities and references:* Estate of Luedke, 65 Wis.2d 387, 222 N.W.2d 643 (1974); Kunde v. Kunde, 52 Wis.2d 559, 191 N.W.2d 41 (1971); In Re Beat's Estate, 25 Wis.2d 315, 130 N.W.2d 739 (1964); In Re Harris' Estate, 7 Wis.2d 417, 96 N.W.2d 718 (1959); In Re Knippel's Estate, 7 Wis.2d 335, 96 N.W.2d 514 (1959); Fricke v. Fricke, 257 Wis. 124, 42 N.W.2d 500 (1950); In Re Koeffler's Will, 218 Wis. 560, 260 N.W. 638 (1935), reh. denied 218 Wis. 560, 261 N.W. 711; In Re Koeffler's Estate, 215 Wis. 115, 254 N.W. 363 (1934); In Re Shirley's Will, 207 Wis. 549, 242 N.W. 207 (1932); Bibelhausen v. Bibelhausen, 159 Wis. 365, 150 N.W. 516 (1915); Ryan v. Dockery, 134 Wis. 431, 114 N.W. 820 (1910).

Wyoming

1. *General comment:* Wyoming allows PREMAs under the rules relating to fairness and disclosure applied throughout the jurisdictions.

Wyoming has limited case law on point.

2. *Divorce contingency provision allowed?* Unknown.

3. *Common-law marriage state?* No.

4. *Community property state?* No.

5. *Legal authorities and references:* Wyoming Statutes, Section 2-37; In Re Borton's Estate, 393 P.2d 808 (Wyo. 1964); Metz v. Blackburn, 9 Wyo. 481, 65 P. 857.

District of Columbia

1. *General comment:* The District of Columbia allows PREMAs under the general rules relating to fairness and disclosure recognized throughout the jurisdictions. If the agreement puts one of the spouses at a disadvantage, then the favored spouse must show that the other signed freely and voluntarily and with adequate knowledge of the favored spouse's assets.

2. *Divorce contingency provision allowed?* Yes, although the District of Columbia Court of Appeals has stated that it recognizes that the parties to such an agreement have likely not been dealing at arm's

length, and that therefore such agreements will be scrutinized more carefully than ordinary contracts.

3. *Common-law marriage jurisdiction?* Yes.

4. *Community property jurisdiction?* No.

5. *Legal authorities and references:* District of Columbia Code, Sections 16-910 and 19-113; Burtoff v. Burtoff, 418 A.2d 1085 (D.C.App. 1980); Brice v. Brice, 411 A.2d 340 (D.C.App. 1980); Mitchell v. Mitchell, 310 A.2d 837 (Dist.Col.App. 1973); Posnick v. Posnick, 225 F.2d 37, 96 U.S.App.D.C. 198 (1955); Pollock v. Jameson, 63 App.D.C. 152, 70 F.2d 756 (1934).

Appendix 3. Uniform Premarital Agreement Act

Section 1. DEFINITIONS

As used in this Act:

(1) "Premarital agreement" means an agreement between prospective spouses made in contemplation of marriage and to be effective upon marriage.

(2) "Property" means an interest, present or future, legal or equitable, vested or contingent, in real or personal property, including income and earnings.

Section 2. FORMALITIES

A premarital agreement must be in writing and signed by both spouses. It is enforceable without consideration.

Section 3. CONTENT

(a) Parties to a premarital agreement may contract with respect to:

    (1) the rights and obligations of each of the parties in any of the property of either or both of them whenever and wherever acquired or located;

    (2) the right to buy, sell, use, transfer, exchange, abandon, lease, consume, expend, assign, create a security interest in, mortgage, encumber, dispose of, or otherwise manage and control property;

    (3) the disposition of property upon separation, marital dissolution, death, or the occurrence or nonoccurrence of any other event;

    (4) the modification or elimination of spousal support;

    (5) the making of a will, trust, or other arrangement to carry out the provisions of the agreement;

(6) the ownership of rights in and disposition of the death benefit from a life insurance policy;

(7) the choice of law governing the construction of the agreement; and

(8) any other matter, including their personal rights and obligations, not in violation of public policy or a statute imposing a criminal penalty.

(b) The right of a child to support may not be adversely affected by a premarital agreement.

Section 4. EFFECT OF MARRIAGE

A premarital agreement becomes effective upon marriage.

Section 5. AMENDMENT, REVOCATION

After marriage, a premarital agreement may be amended or revoked only by a written agreement signed by the parties. The amended agreement or the revocation is enforceable without consideration.

Section 6. ENFORCEMENT

(a) A premarital agreement is not enforceable if the party against whom enforcement is sought proves that:

(1) that party did not execute the agreement voluntarily; or

(2) the agreement was unconscionable when it was executed and, before execution of the agreement, that party:

(i) was not provided a fair and reasonable disclosure of the property or financial obligations of the other party;

(ii) did not voluntarily and expressly waive, in writing, any right to disclosure of the property or financial obligations of the other party beyond the disclosure provided; and

(iii) did not have, or reasonably could not have had, an adequate knowledge of the property or financial obligations of the other party.

(b) If a provision of a premarital agreement modifies or eliminates spousal support and that modification or elimination causes one party to the agreement to be eligible for support under a program of public assistance at the time of separation or marital dissolution, a court, notwithstanding the terms of the agreement, may require the other party to provide support to the extent necessary to avoid that eligibility.

(c) An issue of unconscionability of a premarital agreement shall be decided by the court as a matter of law.

Section 7. ENFORCEMENT: VOID MARRIAGE

If a marriage is determined to be void, an agreement that would otherwise have been a premarital agreement is enforceable to the extent necessary to avoid an inequitable result.

Section 8. LIMITATION OF ACTIONS

Any statute of limitations applicable to an action asserting a claim for relief under a premarital agreement is tolled during the marriage of the parties to the agreement. However, equitable defenses limiting the time for enforcement, including latches and estoppel, are available to either party.

Section 9. APPLICATION AND CONSTRUCTION

This Act shall be applied and construed to effectuate its general purpose to make uniform the law with respect to the subject of this Act among states enacting it.

Section 10. SHORT TITLE

This Act may be cited as the Uniform Premarital Agreement Act.

Section 11. SEVERABILITY

If any provision of this Act or its application to any person or circumstance is held invalid, the invalidity does not affect other provisions or applications of this Act which can be given effect without the invalid provision or application, and to this end the provisions of this Act are severable.

Section 12. TIME OF TAKING EFFECT

This Act takes effect _____ and applies to any premarital agreement executed on or after that date.

Section 13. REPEAL. . . .

Note: The Uniform Premarital Agreement Act was drafted by the Uniform Conference of Commissioners on Uniform State Laws in July 1983, and recommended by the commissioners for approval in all states. Such recommendation is not binding on the states, and at this time it is too early to determine how many states will adopt the Act. Because of the fact that the Act's provisions are contrary to precedent and the declared public policy in some states, it seems certain that its provisions will not be enacted verbatim throughout the jurisdictions, but presently about a dozen state legislatures are considering adoption of the Act. Those state legislatures are as follows: Arkansas, Hawaii, Idaho, Kansas, Maine, Massachusetts, Minnesota, Montana, New Jersey, Oklahoma, Rhode Island, South Dakota, and West Virginia.

Thanks is extended to the Uniform Conference of Commissioners on Uniform State Laws (645 North Michigan Avenue, Suite 510, Chicago, Illinois 60611) for permission to reprint the Act in this book.

Index

Index

151